FINANCIAL SECTOR OF THE AMERICAN ECONOMY

edited by

STUART BRUCHEY
UNIVERSITY OF MAINE

A GARLAND SERIES

THE GROWTH OF INTRA-INDUSTRY TRADE

NEW TRADE PATTERNS IN A CHANGING GLOBAL ECONOMY

LÉONIE L. STONE

GARLAND PUBLISHING, INC.
NEW YORK & LONDON / 1997

M   Library of Congress Cataloging-in-Publication Data

Stone, Léonie L., 1960–
    The growth of intra-industry trade : new trade patterns in a
changing global economy / Léonie L. Stone.
       p.   cm. — (Financial sector of the American economy)
    Includes bibliographical references and index.
    ISBN 0-8153-2874-5 (alk. paper)
    1. International trade—Econometric models. 2. Competition,
International—Econometric models. 3. Commercial policy—
Econometric models. 4. Manufacturing industries—Econometric
models. I. Title. II. Series.
HF1379.S764 1997
382—dc21
                                                              97-10596

Printed on acid-free, 250-year-life paper
Manufactured in the United States of America

For Paul, who is *still* very patient,
and Jonathan, who tries to be.

Contents

List of Tables

List of Figures

Preface

This work began ten years ago with an area of research in which I became interested as a Ph.D. candidate at the Ohio State University. It has continued through the years and through much frustration, largely due to the inadequacy of world data collection, to be of primary scholarly interest to me. While this effort seems to me to be only a small step toward exploration of this subject, my hope is that others interested in the field will be able to gain some knowledge here.

I would like to thank all of those who contributed to this and my other academic efforts, including Edward J. Ray, Patricia Reagan, Paul Evans, and Steven Beckman, as well as the many conference participants and discussants who have added depth to various parts of this work.

A number of my students and research assistants contributed to the data collection and the construction of this book, particularly Teague Ruder (a superior proofreader), Richard Kirk, Anita Lopez and Emily Pleger. Kathy Ackerman provided superior typing assistance and general help. Remaining errors are, unfortunately, my own.

The Growth of
Intra-Industry Trade

I

Introduction

The explosive growth of world trade in the last three decades is unparalleled in history, both due to the rapid increase in volume and to the change in the composition of trade. Historically, trade between nations has consisted largely of exchanges of products that were very different from each other, neither closely substitutable in consumption nor production processes. This type of trade usually arises from the resource endowment differences between countries and resulting unequal production costs. Thus the observed factor content of a country's imports and exports tended to be very different. However, in this latest period of trade expansion, the majority of the increase in world trade has been in manufactured goods, many of which are highly substitutable differentiated products. This has led to growth in intra-industry trade, the cross-shipment of similar products.

Neoclassical trade theories, such as the fundamental Heckscher-Ohlin model, are based on this assumption of differing national factor endowments and costs. In general, they cannot predict or explain intra-industry trade, because in such models, there is no reason for countries to trade identical products. Foreign products would simply be identical to domestic goods but more expensive.

Consequently, a number of theoretical models of intra-industry trade have been developed. These models have explained the phenomenon on the basis of monopolistically competitive world markets producing intermediate or final products which are differentiated in some manner, and whose production involves some type of scale economies. Consumers, whose demand structures are assumed to include a taste for variety, will purchase some of each good, and thus there is intra-industry trade. Unlike classical theories, these models focus on the increasing similarities between nations rather than on endowment differences.

Related empirical investigations have explored the determinants of intra-industry trade in any given year, but there has been no continuous study of the process over time. Cross-sectional studies provide evidence of the effects of exogenous variables on some endogenous variable at one moment in time. The results of such studies can be used to make inferences about the evolution of economic systems over time only if the variables are actually observed in long run equilibrium. If this assumption is not justifiable, it is not clear what is actually known about dynamic changes in intra-industry trade, based on the results of such studies.

The major conclusions of cross-sectional studies are that increased intra-industry trade is associated with similar per capita incomes, similar levels of development, and similar economic sizes. The primary objective of this study is to evaluate the extent to which these conclusions are borne out over time.

For example, a number of cross-sectional studies have found that intra-industry trade is highest among countries with similar levels of development. However, we do not know from this observation if the proportion of intra-industry trade would necessarily increase as countries become more similar. This study provides strong evidence that this relationship does exist over long periods of time.

Secondly, while hypotheses as to the effects of relative factor endowments have figured prominently in the more recent theoretical literature, most longitudinal studies have not explicitly included capital/labor ratios as an independent variable. Therefore, the influence of demand-side changes in level of development or relative incomes could not be distinguished from supply-side changes in relative endowments. This important omission is corrected here.

Finally, while data availability limits the scope of such work, this study links increased shares of intra-industry trade with growth in newly-industrializing countries. While no precise direction of causality can be determined given the existing data, the correlation suggests targets for development policies. Consideration of such policies and their effects on intra-industry trade may help to explain why some nations have succeeded in achieving high growth rates while similar countries have lagged behind.

Improved understanding of long-run trends in intra-industry trade is vital as increased emphasis is placed on strategic trade policy and the management of trade. The presence of intra-industry trade can lead to different policy prescriptions than those of classical theory; thus, as the world economy becomes more integrated, any strategic analysis must consider the reasons for the growth of intra-industry trade. Trade barriers and their effectiveness and desirability must also be reconsidered in this light.

To examine these questions, this study first gives a review of existing literature, both theoretical and empirical. Five hypotheses on intra-industry trade are then discussed. A model is then presented and estimated, using data on bilateral trade between the United States and its five major trading partners, Canada, Japan, France, Germany, and the United Kingdom. A broader sample, consisting of Australia, Belgium, Brazil, Canada, Finland, France, Germany, Greece, Ireland, Israel, Italy, Japan, Korea, Mexico, the Netherlands, New Zealand, Norway, Portugal, Spain, Sweden, the United Kingdom, and Venezuela is then studied, and the correlation between income growth and growth in the share of intra-industry trade is considered. Finally, the results are summarized, and policy applications and directions of future research are examined.

II

Review of Theoretical Literature

A variety of theoretical models have been developed to explain intra-industry trade. The greatest difference between these models is the initial assumption as to the type of market structure in which intra-industry trade takes place. While this study focuses primarily on intra-industry trade in structurally competitive markets, the following presents an overview of the types of models found in the literature.

2.1 STRUCTURALLY COMPETITIVE MODELS

Structurally competitive markets are assumed to exist in industries in which there are no barriers to entry and many firms, all of which earn zero profits in equilibrium. However, models vary as to assumptions about the type of product differentiation that exists. Greenaway and Milner (1986)[1] separate models of intra-industry trade in such markets into three types, neo-Heckscher-Ohlin, neo-Hotelling, and neo-Chamberlinian.

Neo-Heckscher-Ohlin models developed in Falvey (1981) and extended in Falvey and Kierzkowski (1987) assume a world in which countries may have different factor endowments, and thus "traditional" trade, based on comparative advantage, can exist. However, it is assumed that capital is specific to industries and that at least one industry produces a vertically (quality) differentiated product. Differentiation is determined by the capital-labor ratio in that industry, and demand for each variety is a function of relative prices and consumer incomes. Intra-industry trade will occur in this setting as the capital-abundant country produces higher quality varieties and trades for lower quality varieties. This model explains trade in vertically (quality) differentiated products. However, it has been argued that this type of trade, which involves the cross-shipping of items that are classified in the same industry but are probably not close substitutes in consumption, such as Fords and Ferraris, is more of a categorical aggregation problem than an observation of true intra-industry trade.

The issue of product differentiation and what type of differentiation is important to intra-industry trade is continually discussed in both this and in the related industrial organization literature. Underlying the entire discussion is the highly problematic theoretical question of what makes a product differentiated but not different. The only apparent empirical solution to this lies in finer disaggregation of industry classifications. While no new solutions are suggested here, it is important to keep this caveat in mind when viewing what may only appear to be intra-industry trade due to categorical aggregation or misdefined industries.

In all other models of structurally competitive markets, it is assumed that the industry structure is monopolistically competitive due to the existence of some type of scale economy. The most comprehensive models of these processes may be found in Helpman and Krugman (1985), which synthesizes the neo-Hotelling and neo-Chamberlinian approaches, and in Bergstrand (1989,1990), which use gravity equation models.

In neo-Chamberlinian models, of which Krugman (1979, 1981, 1982) is most notable, production of horizontally differentiated products is characterized by internal scale economies. [2] Each firm has some non-zero fixed cost and constant marginal costs, and there are no barriers to entry. Thus, in equilibrium, profits must be zero as firms will enter the market when positive profits exist. Consumers prefer variety and therefore gain from increased product differentiation, as all commodities enter the utility function symmetrically. Where countries' factor endowments are alike, trade will be intra-industry in nature. If endowments are dissimilar, trade will follow Heckscher-Ohlin patterns.

Ethier (1979, 1982)[3] develops models of intra-industry trade in intermediate goods in which both internal and external scale economies affect production. Firms may experience both scale economies related to plant size and economies related to increased (world-wide) specialization, the latter depending on the size of the world market. These models are analogous to Krugman in that all intermediate goods enter the final manufacture symmetrically, and thus there is demand for each variety. Intermediate goods markets are assumed to be perfectly competitive but experience external economies of scale associated with the size of the market. Intra-industry trade again results when countries have similar endowments and thus similarly-sized markets.

Closely related to these models are neo-Hotelling models such as Lancaster (1980) and Helpman (1981). The principal difference between these and the Krugman and Ethier is the specification of the utility function. Products are viewed as bundles of characteristics, and there are assumed to be an infinite number of different varieties possible. Each customer has some most-preferred variety, which may or may not be actually produced. The price that the consumer will pay depends on the distance between the variety in question and the most-preferred variety.[4] Firms again experience internal economies of scale, and the market may be characterized as monopolistically competitive. Each firm is assumed to produce only one commodity. In autarky, the no-trade equilibrium, if the distribution of types of consumers is not identical across countries, different varieties will be produced in different parts of the world. With the opening of trade, intra-industry trade arises because some consumers' most-preferred varieties are being produced elsewhere. Even if the distribution of consumers is identical across countries, the opening of trade will allow the production of some varieties not previously produced, as the size of the market (the number of consumers of each type) has increased. These models have also been extended to allow for differences in factor endowments. While the results of these models are extremely similar to the Krugman studies above, the formulation of the utility function is more intuitively appealing.

Helpman and Krugman (1985) present a synthesized model which combines the approaches or allows for alternative formulations of some functions. The following presents much of the detail of this model as later hypotheses will be based on its conclusions. The following discussion refers throughout to Helpman and Krugman (1985) and Helpman (1987); the reader is referred to these works for further detail on the derivation of the models. Only the 2 x 2 x 2 model is presented here, but this may easily be extended to a many factor, many good world.

Assume a two country, two factor (K,L), two-good (X,Y) world in which consumers in both countries have identical, homothetic preferences. Utility is represented as:

$$U = U[u_1 (.), u_2 (.),...,u_I (.)] \tag{2.1}$$

Thus each u_i (.) represents subutility from consumption of product i; $U(.)$, assumed homothetic in its arguments, combines all subutility functions to yield the overall level of utility. Subutilities are assumed to depend only on the total quantity consumed if the product is homogeneous but on the quantity of *each* variety consumed if the good is differentiated. This implies the preference for variety that drives this type of model.[5]

One simple formulation of the subutility functions is to assume constant elasticity of substitution; the representative household will then maximize utility by consuming equal amounts of all varieties of each good, assuming that there is an identical price for each variety.

All production functions exhibit constant returns to scale. Asterisks denote foreign country variables. Consider the integrated equilibrium in this world, defined as "the resource allocation the world would have if goods and factors were both perfectly mobile."[6]

In general, this allocation may be achieved even without factor mobility as long as endowments fall within some range, defined as the factor price equalization (FPE) set. It is assumed that, for endowments within the FPE set, in the free trade equilibrium with full employment, production techniques will be the same as in the integrated equilibrium.

The FPE set is then a convex combination of the sectoral employment vectors, defined in the integrated equilibrium by cost-minimizing production in competitive markets. Good X is assumed to use a more capital-intensive production process. Geometrically, this world can be represented by Figure 1, where 0Q (0*Q') is the home (foreign) vector of employment in sector X, Q0* (Q'0) is the home (foreign) vector of employment in sector Y, and resulting parallelogram is the FPE set.

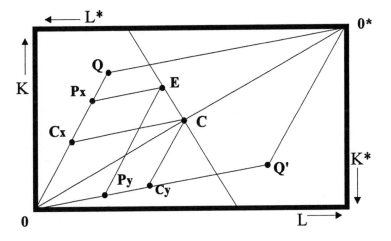

Figure 1: Location of production and consumption points.

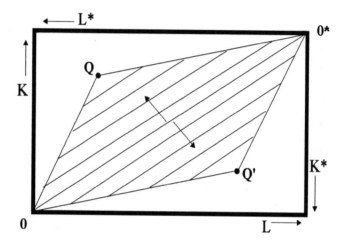

Figure 2: Iso-volume-of-trade curves with homogeneous goods.

Assume initially that both goods are homogeneous, that there is no intra-industry trade in homogeneous goods, and that the home country is relatively capital-rich. In this simple world, the home country will export X and import Y. The nominal volume of trade, defined as the sum of each nation's exports, is then:

$$V = p_x (X - sX^W) + p_y (Y^* - s^*Y^W) \qquad (2.2)$$

where X (X^*) is the output of X in the home (foreign) country, Y (Y^*) is the output of Y in the home (foreign) country, X^W (Y^W) is the world output of X (Y), and s (s*) is the share of the home (foreign) country in world spending.

If trade is balanced, then:

$$V = 2p (X - sX^W) = 2 p (Y^* - s^*Y^W) \qquad (2.3)$$

In Figure 1, E is the endowment point, and C is the consumption point, located by tracing through E a line with the slope $(-w_l/w_k)$, where w_l, w_k are the factor rewards found in the integrated equilibrium and thus also in the trading equilibrium. C is located at the point at which this line intersects the diagonal, and this divides the diagonal into segments representing relative share of world income. Let $0Q=X^W$ (total world production of X), $Q0^*=Y^W$ (total world production of Y), and $00^*=$GDP (world gross domestic product in the integrated equilibrium). Then the home country's production and consumption points are found by constructing parallelograms at E and C, and it is clear that X is exported and Y is imported. With full employment, $0P_x$ is employed in industry X; $0P_y$ is employed in industry Y.

Within the FPE set, if both goods are homogeneous, it may be shown from the above that the volume of trade is constant along straight lines parallel to the diagonal 00^* (Figure 2). These iso-volume-of-trade curves depend only on the relative endowments, with the maximum volume of trade occurring when endowments are most dissimilar within the FPE set. As the difference in endowments increases, the volume of trade rises (shown geometrically as a move away from the diagonal). However, a change in endowments that changes relative income but preserves capital-labor ratios does not change the volume of trade.

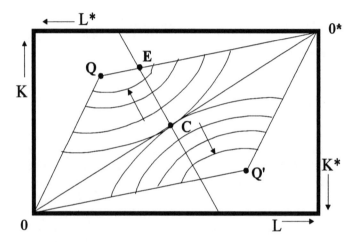

Figure 3: Iso-volume-of-trade curves, X differentiated,
Y homogeneous.

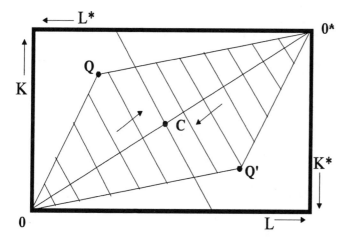

Figure 4: Iso-volume-of-trade, both goods differentiated.

Now assume that X is a differentiated good produced with identical, decreasing-cost technology. As free entry and exit is assumed, there will be number of firms in equilibrium, each making zero profits. Every variety is assumed to be priced identically and thus produced in the same quantity. Again, the home country imports Y and exports X.

The home country remains a net exporter of X. However, as some of the firms producing X will be located in the foreign country, there will thus be intra-industry trade, as consumers in each country desire some of each variety of X. Now, where x is the zero- profit output of each firm and n^W is the number of firms in the world:

$$X^W = xn^W \tag{2.4}$$

As the value of exports of differentiated goods from the home country is (s^*p_x nx) and the value of exports of differentiated goods from the foreign country is now (sp_x n*x), the volume of trade is:

$$V = s^*p_x \, nx + sp_x \, n^*x + p_y(Y^* - sY^W) \tag{2.5}$$

Or, if balanced trade is assumed, the volume of trade reduces to:

$$V = 2s^*p_x \, nx \tag{2.6}$$

Now, the iso-volume-of-trade curves are a function of both relative endowments and relative income (Figure 3); volume of trade is maximized when relative endowments are most dissimilar (within the FPE set) but incomes are equal.

Similarly, it may be shown that if all goods are differentiated, the iso-volume-of- trade curves are again straight lines but parallel to the relative factor reward line ($-w_l/w_k$) rather than to the diagonal; now, relative income is the sole determinant of trade volume (Figure 4). If it is assumed that there is complete specialization, in the sense that no good is produced in more than one country, then the volume of trade reduces to:

$$V = ss^*GDP^W, \tag{2.7}$$

and this will hold even when expanded to a many nation world. As Helpman (1989) observes, this is one theoretical ground for gravity equation models, which are usually a function of each nation's GDP. Such models are discussed later in this section.

Having discussed the basic determinants of the volume of trade in this model, we turn to the determinants of the level and volume of intra-industry trade.

Assume again, for simplicity, that there is only one differentiated good, X, as in Figure 3. Thus the volume of trade is represented by (2.5). The first two terms represent the level of trade in differentiated products; thus the volume of intra-industry trade is:

$$\text{VIIT} = 2 \min (s^* p_x \, nx, \, sp_x \, n^*x) \tag{2.8}$$

The share of intra-industry trade is the ratio of the volume of intra-industry to the volume of trade, which can be reduced to:

$$\text{SIIT} = sX^*/s^*X \tag{2.9}$$

In discussing the static and dynamic properties of this model, it would be possible to specify a system of equations and then derive specific comparative-statics results. However, in order to do this, it is necessary to assume particular functional forms for utility and production functions. While this approach has some appeal in terms of mathematical clarity, it makes the model highly sensitive to the assumptions and results in a large loss of generality. Thus the costs appear to outweigh the benefits at this time. Therefore the following comparative-static discussion is based only on the assumption of identical preferences throughout the world and production technology for good X that exhibits decreasing per-unit costs (increasing returns to scale) over some small scale of output.

It is easily shown that the share of intra-industry trade declines as the disparity in capital/labor ratios rises. See Figure 5. At point E, national incomes and endowment of capital and labor are assumed to be identical. Therefore, both the volume and the share of intra-industry trade are maximized, given world stocks of capital and labor. This is clearly true, first because there is no incentive for intersectoral trade, given identical capital/labor ratios between countries. Secondly, given the assumption of identical preferences, each country must have an equal share in world spending when incomes are equal.

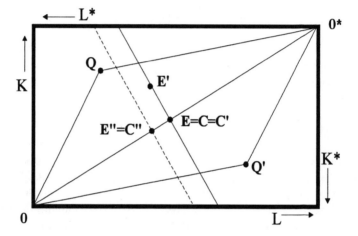

Figure 5: Reallocating capital and labor. Point E' changes
relative endowments but not incomes. Point E" changes
both endowments and incomes.

Now consider a marginal reallocation of capital and labor to E', where incomes remain constant (given the integrated equilibrium wage-rental ratio), but capital and labor are redistributed to make the home country more capital-rich. The X sector in the home country will expand, and the number of firms (n) will rise. The Y sector in the foreign country will rise, and the number of firms producing X (n*) will fall. The volume of intra-industry trade must fall as, in (2.8), n has increased and n* has fallen. As the total number of firms in the world cannot have changed, the effect is the 'relocation' of some X producers to the home country. Since the volume of intra-industry trade fell while the overall volume of trade has risen, the share of intra-industry trade must have declined.

Conversely, any reallocation that preserves capital-labor ratios but changes relative incomes must decrease the level but not the share of intra-industry trade. Consider, in Figure 5, a movement from E to E''. The capital-labor ratio is unchanged but the home country's income has declined relative to the foreign country. Now there is still no incentive for intersectoral trade as capital-labor ratios are still identical throughout the world, and thus the share of intra-industry trade remains equal to one. However, as the home country's income has declined, fewer imports of X can be purchased (given balanced trade), and the level of intra-industry trade must fall.

The above discussion has assumed that capital and labor were simply reallocated. However, in a dynamic world, not only does the distribution of resources changes but their levels are also altered over time. Thus, in this Edgeworth box framework, it is necessary to envision not only movements within the box but changes in the size of the box itself. This presents some conceptual problems, as the integrated equilibrium, which has been used throughout as a reference point, is also changing. For example, begin with a world in which capital and labor is distributed evenly among the two nations, and suppose that endowments of capital and labor in both countries are doubled. It is clear that this type of proportional change would leave capital/labor ratios and relative incomes intact, and would thus change the level but not the share of intra-industry trade.

Similarly, consider an increase in world capital stock without a change in the labor force, and let the increase be distributed equally between the nations. Thus while the world capital/labor ratio, employment vectors, the FPE set, and the wage/rental ratio must have changed, as long as the increase is proportionately distributed, the share of intra-industry trade is still one. Incomes must rise, and as X is the more capital-intensive sector, the production of X must increase more than proportionately. The latter follows from Rybczynski's familiar theorem, which has been shown by Ethier (1982) and others to hold under these production conditions. Thus the level of intra-industry trade, which is a function of the amount of X produced, must rise.

However, what if the amount of capital in the home country increases without a proportionate increase in foreign capital? Now the share of intra-industry trade will be reduced as intersectoral trade takes place, and the home country becomes an importer of Y and a net exporter of X. It is probable that the level of intra-industry trade will also be reduced as the home country is likely to have a higher relative income, but this is uncertain as it depends on the (uncertain) effect on the integrated equilibrium wage/rental ratio.

2.2 A GRAVITY EQUATION MODEL

Bergstrand (1989,1990) develops models based on the so-called gravity equation. The gravity equation has long been used to explain the nominal volume of international trade as an exponential function of gross domestic products (GDP), distance, and other variables related to the trading partners, such as tariff and non-tariff barriers. While a theoretical explanation of this model has been provided by Anderson (1979) and others, this formulation has long been a convenient device for modeling a trade volume equation for easy estimation. The general formulation of this equation is:

$$PX_{ij} = \beta_0 \, (Y_i)^{\beta_1} \, (Y_i/L_i)^{\beta_2} \, (Y_j)^{\beta_3} \, (Y_j/L_j)^{\beta_4} \, (D_{ij})^{\beta_5} \, (A_{ij})^{\beta_6} \, e_{ij} \quad (2.10)$$

where i,j are countries, PX_{ij} is nominal volume of trade between countries i and j, Y is nominal income, L is population, D is distance between economic centers, A is other trade-related factors, and e is a log-normally distributed error term.

Bergstrand provides a microfoundation for the gravity equation based on a general equilibrium model of trade flows, assuming constant elasticity of substitution utility functions and constant elasticity of transformation production functions. This model shows both the factor-endowment basis of the supply side of trade and the influences of incomes and other demand-side factors. The standard index measuring intra-industry trade can easily be derived from this generalized gravity equation. As the mathematical derivation of this model is straightforward but extremely lengthy, the following presents a very brief overview of the method used; the reader is referred to Bergstrand (1989, 1990) for the full model.

Assume a world with two factors, two industries, and many countries. Each household maximizes a nested Cobb-Douglas-CES-Stone-Geary utility function subject to an income constraint; the consumer has Cobb-Douglas preferences over the two goods and a sub-utility function for good X with constant elasticity of substitution (CES). Goods in industry X are differentiated by firm. As in the Helpman/Krugman model, all such goods enter the subutility function symmetrically. Differentiated goods are assumed to be close but imperfect substitutes; however, unlike the Helpman/Krugman model, the overall utility function is not assumed to be homothetic. Goods in industry Z are homogeneous, and the sub-utility function for Z includes a minimum consumption requirement of this good (the standard Stone-Geary formulation). Expenditures are constrained by the consumer's nominal income measured on an aggregate expenditures basis.

Solving for the consumer's constrained maximization problem yields bilateral import demands for each good X as a function of national income, per capita income, import price, transportation cost, tariff rate, exchange rate, prices of other varieties of X, and the elasticity of substitution in consumption (which is assumed to exceed one). As consumers within each country are identical, each country's inverse demand curve for the output of each industry can be derived by aggregating demand curves across consumers.

The output of each firm is viewed as a composite commodity, consisting of product sold domestically and product exported. As in the Krugman/Helpman model, there is a constant marginal cost and a fixed setup cost. Profits are expected to be zero in equilibrium. However, it is further assumed that firms cannot substitute costlessly between domestic and foreign markets. The elasticity of substitution between these markets is assumed to be constant and positive. Solution of the firm's constrained maximization problem yields markup price and total equilibrium output of each firm. The latter is a function of factor prices, marginal input requirements of labor and capital, and consumer elasticity of substitution. The firm's technology is assumed to be linear.

After deriving the associated cost functions, the number of firms in each country can be determined by the relative amounts of capital and labor.

Bergstrand further assumes that each firm's output is distributed among domestic and foreign markets according to a constant elasticity of transformation (CET) function. Maximizing the function yields equations for the marginal cost of exporting to any market.

By treating incomes as exogenous and by making the monopolistic assumption that firms view the marginal utility of income as fixed, it may be shown that the representative firm in industry A will maximize profits by supplying exports in accordance with the marginal cost of exporting.

After making the appropriate substitutions, solving for reduced forms, and summing up across all firms for each industry in each country, we can arrive at what Bergstrand calls the "generalized" gravity equation, which shows the nominal trade flow from one country to another in a particular industry as a function of national incomes, per capita incomes, per unit costs, tariffs, exchange rates, prices, and capital/labor ratios, as well as input prices and the elasticities of substitution and transformation.

Nominal trade flows may then be substituted into the usual formula for bilateral intra-industry trade. The essence of the resulting function is that bilateral intra-industry trade is a function of the above-mentioned determinants of nominal trade flows for each of the pair of countries; the length of the result discourages its inclusion here. For the exact expression for nominal trade flows, the reader is referred to Bergstrand (1990), p. 1220. However, the expression for bilateral intra-industry trade is so lengthy that it was not even printed in the above paper; therefore its omission here is certainly justified. As will be further discussed in Chapter 4, comparative statics results show that the same relationships hypothesized in the Helpman/Krugman model are expected to hold in the Bergstrand model, although in some cases the reasoning is slightly different.

2.3 COMMENTS ON COMPETITIVE MODELS

The Helpman-Krugman and Bergstrand models present carefully formulated and intuitively pleasing explanations of how intra-industry trade can arise in a world with differentiated products but competitive markets.

However, there are a number of problems with the theoretical work on intra-industry trade in competitive markets. First, most models assume that product differentiation is either vertical or horizontal, and this is probably not the case. Gray (1988) argues that the type of differentiation that is relevant is 'gradient,' a combination of horizontal and vertical factors. For example, an automobile is not only differentiated by such (horizontal) characteristics as size and performance but by (vertical) characteristics such as quality. In such a case, the formulations of the utility functions presented are unlikely to capture the true nature of demand for these products, which may be very different in countries with different per capita incomes. Also, much of the related literature suggests that where there is quality differentiation, lower quality variants of the product will tend to be produced in capital-poor countries, possibly using relatively labor-intensive or standardized methods. National income then is a function of which variants are produced; equivalent trade volumes (in the sense of trading equal number of the product) do not imply equivalent revenues.

Secondly, the direction of trade (particularly in the sense of which countries produce which varieties of the product) is usually indeterminate.

Third, the models must, for manageability, assume constant so many of the realities of observed intra-industry trade that the results do not generate useful predictions that correspond with observation and do not lend themselves to the derivation of testable empirical models. Also, since the differences between these models lie largely in assumptions, with few distinctive, testable implications, it is difficult or impossible for empirical results to distinguish between them and thus offer support for one specification versus another. This complaint is made by both Greenaway and Milner (1986) and Gray (1988).

Fourth, the dynamics of intra-industry trade have not been modeled successfully. As some argue that the most relevant type of scale economies involved derives from dynamic increasing returns such as learning-by-doing, this area should be a focal point for future theoretical research .

2.4 IMPERFECTLY COMPETITIVE MARKETS

A large portion of the literature has been devoted to intra-industry trade in markets that are not structurally competitive; in such markets intra-industry trade is usually assumed to result from the strategic interaction of monopolistic firms located in different countries. This interaction has been modeled in a Cournot framework by Brander (1981) and Brander and Krugman (1983). Intra-industry trade here consists not of trade in differentiated products but rather "reciprocal dumping" of identical goods in foreign markets.

Models involving both vertical and horizontal differentiation of products have also been developed. Shaked and Sutton (1982, 1983, 1984) study markets in which products are quality-differentiated; firms face a three-part decision process. Fixed costs vary with quality; firms must decide whether to enter, which quality to produce, and what price to charge. Demand for each quality depends on the distribution of consumer incomes. As in Falvey's model above, when trade is opened, there will be a greater number and type of consumers available. Thus more qualities can be profitably produced, and intra-industry trade is the result.

In Eaton and Kierzkowski (1983), products are horizontally differentiated, and each consumer has some most-preferred variety, as in the neo-Hotelling models above. Firms again face a sequential decision-making process, choosing entry, variety, and price. However, there may or may not be an increased number of firms with trade, depending on the distribution of consumers and income.

All of the above models assume that each firm produces one and only one variety (or quality) of product. Some work has been done on the issue of multinational, multi-product firms. Greenaway (1982) discusses multi-product firms; a number of studies such as Agmon (1979), Agmon and Hirsch (1979), and Mainardi (1986) consider multinational firms. In these models, intra-industry trade generally develops for strategic reasons, as in the oligopolistic models. Multi-product firms may export due to cost advantages over potential domestic entrants (their start-up costs in the home market are already sunk). Multinationals may export as part of a learning process prior to foreign direct investment. This literature, as well as Ethier (1982), Helpman (1981), and Norman and Dunning (1984), also explores the interesting question of the role of factor movements and intra-industry trade. In traditional models, factor mobility and trade are substitutes; if there is free trade, factor mobility is irrelevant as factor prices will equalize throughout the world.

However, it has often been hypothesized that the extent of intra-industry trade increases with similarity of factor endowments. Thus any factor movements that serve to increase the similarity of factor endowments should increase intra-industry trade. Additionally, if multinationals do use intra-industry trade to gain information about foreign markets prior to investing, intra-industry trade and factor mobility should again be complementary.

The chief criticism of imperfect competition models is identical to that of most game-theoretic work. The models rest heavily on specific assumptions about behavior and are not robust if these assumptions are changed even slightly (or tend to yield an embarrassment of equilibria). For example, even in the simple, homogeneous-goods cases, results depend almost entirely on the assumptions on conjectural variation, the modeling of which has presented continuing problems in the industrial organization literature. Thus even if these models do reflect the state of the world, they have limited usefulness in terms of economic theory or prediction.

NOTES

[1] The general structure of the following discussion owes much to this excellent survey of research on intra-industry trade.

[2] Horizontal differentiation refers to products that are essentially of the same quality but which possess different characteristics, such as brands of breakfast cereal.

[3] See also Dixit and Norman (1980), Venables (1984), and Lawrence and Spiller (1983).

[4] Lancaster models the distribution of customers and goods along a straight line while Helpman places them on a circle; the qualitative results are similar between specifications.

[5] See Helpman and Krugman (1985), Chapter 6, for further discussion of how preference for variety may be modeled.

[6] See Helpman and Krugman, Chapter 1, as well as Dixit and Norman (1980), for full discussion of the integrated equilibrium.

III

Empirical Studies of Intra-Industry Trade

In recent years, the empirical work on intra-industry trade has multiplied. However, the proliferation of research has not been able to achieve any true consensus on its determinants.

Studies have centered on either country-specific or industry-specific determinants. Industry-specific determinants of intra-industry trade explain an industry's proportion of such trade on the basis of differences in country and industry infrastructures. These infrastructure variations include product differentiation (or standardization), scale economies, industry-specific transportation costs (such as average shipment distance within the country), offshore assembly provisions, size of foreign market, marketing costs, export concentration ratios, and degree of aggregation. The country-specific view explains intra-industry trade through average levels of macroeconomic variables in each country, such as per capita income and capital/labor ratio differences.

This chapter presents an overview of the variety of industry-specific cross-sectional studies and then focuses attention on the country-specific literature that is most closely related to this study.

3.1 INDUSTRY STUDIES

The bulk of empirical research on intra-industry trade consists of cross-sectional examinations which are largely industry-specific in focus. Overall, these studies have used similar variables but have obtained differing results. Much of the difference appears to have arisen from the use of a variety of proxy variables across studies.

Additionally, there are some question as to the probable effects of certain variables.

As previously noted, industry-specific determinants of intra-industry trade explain an industry's proportion of such trade on the basis of differences in country and industry infrastructures. These infrastructure variations include product differentiation (or standardization), scale economies, industry-specific transportation costs (such as average shipment distance within the country), offshore assembly provisions, size of foreign markets, marketing costs, export concentration ratios, and degree of aggregation. The dependent variable is an index of intra-industry trade, measured bilaterally or multilaterally, with or without adjustment for trade imbalances. Many of the problems with empirical studies seem to lie with difficulties in defining the exogenous variables.

For example, a number of methods have been used to determine product differentiation: coefficient of determination of export unit values (Hufbauer, 1970); hedonic price indices (Gray and Martin, 1980); research and development, support costs, selling costs, foreign direct investment, standard deviation of profit rates, and advertising costs (Caves, Balassa). None of these variables is completely satisfactory, especially because in some cases, it is not clear exactly what is being measured by these proxies. Also, in some studies more than one proxy is used, and it is likely that, if these variables are actually measuring product differentiation, there is a high degree of collinearity.

Additionally, it is not clear what type of product differentiation is relevant in these cases. As noted in the previous chapter, Gray (1988) distinguishes differentiation as horizontal (differences in product characteristics), vertical (differences in quality and cost), and gradient (a combination of vertical and horizontal differentiation) and claims that the third is most relevant to intra-industry trade. However, in most studies, no measures of this type of differentiation have been attempted, and the difficulties involved in finding a proxy are considerable. More recent studies (Greenaway et al, (1995), Abed-el-Rahman (1991)) are beginning to measure quality differentiation through price differences; this emerging literature is not fully discussed here pending further developments.

Similar problems exist with the measurement of scale economies, in part due to the basic disagreement as to the type of scale economies that are important to intra-industry trade. Some studies use measures of internal scale economies while others proxy external economies. Internal scale economies are decreases in per unit costs as the firm attains greater scales of production, and such cost savings clearly accrue only to that firm. External economies are per unit cost reductions that accrue to all firms in the industry as the size of the entire industry increases. Most studies use only variables that attempt to measure internal economies, even though some of the theoretical models are based on external economies.

Finally, Bergstrand (1983) contends that the extent of returns to scale increases with product differentiation; thus one but not both of these variables should appear in the model. This criticism, if correct, has been almost universally ignored.

As most of these studies use different years, countries, and levels of aggregation, as well as the previously noted differences in exogenous variables, direct comparison is problematic. Goodness-of-fit measures are also not comparable as a number of estimation procedures have been used, including ordinary, weighted, and nonlinear least squares (OLS, WLS, NLLS). Even so, it should be noted that there is a large amount of difference in goodness-of-fit of these models; for example, R^2 values range from a low of .07 (Loertscher and Wolter) to a high of .94 (Balassa).

Table 1 lists year of publication and author(s) for twelve representative industry studies. Table 2 shows year(s), country(ies), type of trade flows, level of aggregation, and sample size for these studies. The majority of studies use United States trade, followed by some number of OECD nations. Only Tharakan (1984) and Balassa (1986) devote special attention to less-developed countries (LDCs). Most studies have used the 3-digit level of aggregation, but increasingly the four-digit level has been chosen, presumably reducing the bias due to categorical aggregation. All of these studies have concentrated on manufacturing industries.

Table 3 identifies the proxy variables used in the above studies. Table 4 defines these variables. Most studies have used one or more measures of product differentiation and scale economies; other variables differ.

TABLE 1: Selected cross-sectional studies	Author(s)	Year
1	Pagoulatos/ Sorenson	1975
2	Finger/DeRosa	1979
3	Loertscher/Wolter	1980
4	Caves	1981
5	Lundberg	1982
6	Toh	1982
7	Bergstrand	1983
8	Greenaway/Milner	1984
9	Tharakan	1984
10	Balassa	1986
11	Marvel/Ray	1987
12	Ray	1990

TABLE 2: Specifications of selected cross-sectional studies					
Study	Year(s)	Countries	Trade Flows	Level	Size
1	65,67	USA	multilateral	3 digit	102
2	63,67, 72,75	USA	trade with 13 nations	3 digit	75
3	71,72	OECD	bilateral	3 digit	59
4	70	14 OECD	trade within industry group	3 digit	94
5	70,77	Sweden	multilateral	4 digit	77
6	70,71	USA	multilateral	4 digit	112
7	76	14 OECD	bilateral	2 digit	3
8	77	U.K.	multilateral	3 digit	68
9	72,73, 74	5 industrial	trade with LDC's	3 digit	102
10	79	18 developed 20 LDC	bilateral	4 digit	167
11	72	USA	multilateral	3 digit	314
12	84	USA	multilateral	3 digit	195

TABLE 3:
Proxy variables in selected cross-sectional studies

	TO	PD	ES	MS	TF	DS	TB	FDI
1	1	1,2	3	--	--	2	--	--
2	--	2	1	--	3	--	--	--
3	1	1	1	--	--	2	--	--
4	--	1,2,3,4	1	--	1	2	1	1,2
5	3	2	--	1,2	--	--	--	--
6	1	2	2	2,3	3	2	1,2	--
7	2	--	3	2,3	--	1,3	1	--
8	1	1,4	1	1	1	--	--	--
9	1	1	1	--	--	2	--	--
10	1	--	4	--	--	1,3	--	--
11	--	4,5,6	3,4	1	4	--	--	--
12	--	4,5,6	3,4	1	4	--	--	--

TABLE 4: Definitions of proxy variables	
TO: *Taste Overlap*	1: difference in per capita incomes or similarity in per capita incomes 2: other taste difference proxy
PD: *Product Differentiation*	1: number of product groups or tariff positions for each 'industry' 2: Hufbauer index (variation of export unit values) 3: input into sales activities 4: advertising/sales ratio 5: consumer goods ratio 6: sectoral dispersion index or other measure of specialization
ES: *Economies of scale*	1: relative value added or minimum efficient scale 2: length of production run or share of labor force in large plants 3: scale factor, capital/labor ratios 4: midpoint plant shipments
MS: *Market structure*	1: four or five firm concentration ratio 2: international concentration ratio 3: entry barriers for foreign firms
TF: *Technological factors*	1: research and development 2: technical personnel/ labor force 3: rate of product variety or turnover 4: inventory ratio
DS: *Distance*	1: physical distance between partners 2: distance shipped in the U.S. 3: common border dummy variable
TB: *Trade barriers*	1: industry average nominal tariffs 2: non-tariff barriers
FDI: *Foreign Direct Investment*	1: extent of foreign investment activity 2: importance in trade of exchange between US multinationals and foreign affiliates

3.2 COUNTRY STUDIES

The variety of studies by Balassa (1986a,b,c,) and Balassa and Bauwens (1985, 87, 88), as well as Bergstrand (1983) and Loertscher and Wolter (1980), take a largely country-specific approach. This view of intra-industry trade is fundamentally different from the cross-sectional studies. In country studies, intra-industry trade is explained by average levels of variables in each country. This view is attractive for a number of reasons. First, the variables used to explain inter-country differences, such as income levels as proxy for extent of the market, tend not to require the elaborate construction that many industry-specific studies use.

Secondly, these studies have implications relating to differences between nations at different levels of development and income growth and may offer policy prescriptions for the future. Industry studies, which yield results specific to industries rather than nations, are less useful in this area.

Finally, the theoretical models of country-specific determinants, as discussed above, are far better developed. For theoretical grounding, many industry-specific studies rely on largely ad hoc assumptions about variables that 'should' affect such trade, and it is difficult to find adequate proxies for many of the assumed relationships.

Overall, studies have used similar variables but have attained differing results. As most of these studies use different years, countries, and levels of aggregation, as well as a variety of estimation methods, direct comparison of the quantitative results is difficult. The majority of studies use United States trade and some or all of the OECD nations. Most studies have used the 3-digit level of aggregation, but increasingly the four-digit level has been chosen, presumably reducing the bias due to categorical aggregation. While some studies have used multilateral trade levels, it can be shown that multilateral intra-industry trade is not inconsistent with a Heckscher-Ohlin world, but that bilateral flows cannot be explained. Therefore, bilateral intra-industry trade is the more interesting phenomenon.

In the last fifteen years, there have been a number of country-specific or combined industry/country studies. As the methods and models of most of these studies are very similar, only Balassa (1986c), Helpman (1987), and Bergstrand (1990) will be discussed in detail here.

Balassa (1986c) considers a sample consisting of both developed and developing nations. The share of intra-industry trade is modeled as a function of log of average per capita income, the difference in per capita incomes, log of average income, weighted difference in income, a trade orientation index, and dummy variables for common border, language, and economic integration. As the motivation for this choice of variables is very similar to that discussed in Chapter 4 of this study, it is omitted here.

The relationship is estimated by non-linear least squares, and the results show statistically significant relationships and the expected signs at the 1% level of significance for all variables with the exceptions of some of the language and economic integration dummies. The latter is not surprising since most of the nations involved in economic integration plans share a common language, border, or both, and thus the variables may be collinear. The model is also estimated separately for developed and developing countries with similar results. Interestingly, in neither case is the difference in per capita incomes significant. This suggests that, within the two groups of nations, either there is little variation in income or, as argued by Balassa, that demand structures are indeed very similar. Models of this type do not explicitly include factor-endowment variables.

An general criticism of these studies has been leveled by Milner (1988). The standard measure of intra-industry trade, the popular Grubel-Lloyd index, is a variable related (nonlinearly) to the proportion of an industry's trade that is intra-industry. Variants on this index express the amount of intra-industry trade in an industry relative to other industries, and some studies have even used absolute levels of net or gross trade (notably Balassa and Bauwens 1985, 1987, 1988). But when the regression equation is modeled, the relationship between the dependent variable and the explanatory variables has often seemed confused and the difference between changes in the absolute versus the proportional amount of intra-industry trade forgotten. For example, while it should be true that increases in tariff and nontariff barriers have a negative relationship with trade, it is not necessarily clear that these variables would influence intra- more than inter-industry trade. Thus while a negative relationship with the level of intra-industry trade would be expected, the effect on the proportion of intra-industry trade may be uncertain.

Despite numerous studies on country-specific determinants of intra-industry trade, the difficulties involved in the of comparison of results implies that no clear consensus has been achieved on the subject. An additional problem is that all of these studies, even those published very recently, use data from the 1970s. While this is somewhat understandable in light of the colossal collection and comprehension problems involved with this data, these studies omit the rapid growth spurt of trade during the 1960s and the more recent changes in the 1980s. In most cases, these studies simply describe what happened in a single year, more than 15 years ago.

In contrast, Helpman (1987) discusses two hypotheses, that the share of intra-industry trade in the bilateral volume of trade should be larger for countries with similar factor compositions, and that the share of intra-industry trade in the within-group trade volume should be larger the smaller the within-group dispersion in factor composition. These hypotheses are derived from the Helpman/Krugman model as discussed in the previous chapter.

To test these hypotheses, both bilateral and within-group intra-industry trade shares are calculated for 14 countries from 1970-81, using the standard Grubel-Lloyd index. For the bilateral flows in each year, the share of intra-industry trade is regressed on the log of the difference in per capita income (as a proxy for difference in factor compositions), and the logs of the gross domestic products (GDPs) of the two countries. A negative relationship is found between the bilateral share of intra-industry trade and the difference in per capita incomes and also with the size of the larger country; a positive relationship is found between the share of intra-industry trade and the size of the smaller country. These relationships hold in each year, although they are generally not significant in the later periods. A similar equation is used for within-group shares in intra-industry trade; however, in this case, the ratio of the standard deviation of per capita income to its mean is used as a proxy for size dispersion. Intra-industry trade is found to be negatively correlated with size dispersion, but again, the relationship weakens in later years. Thus the results weakly support Helpman's hypotheses.

The chief problem with this study is the choice of income as proxy for factor composition. While, as stated in the paper, this can be used "when there are only two factors of production and goods are freely traded," it is difficult to see how this can be justified here. Thus there is no distinction made between (supply-side) effects of factor composition and (demand-side) effects related to income differences. Secondly, while Helpman tests this relationship in each year and thus has the advantage of covering more years and giving some flavor of the process over time, he does not attempt to estimate any continuous relationship.

Bergstrand (1990), based on the model discussed in the previous section, is the only study to use both income-related and endowments-related variables. As in previous studies, a strong relationship with the standard income-related variables is found. Average capital/labor ratios are also significant, although the difference in capital/labor ratios is not. Methodologically, this study is very similar to Balassa (above); it is most notable for the theoretical model and explicit inclusion of factor endowments

Cross-sectional studies provide evidence of the effects of exogenous variables on some endogenous variable at one moment in time. Thus it is assumed that the variables in question are viewed, at that instant, in their long-run equilibrium state. The results of such studies can be used to make inferences about the evolution of economic systems over time only if the variables are actually observed in long run equilibrium, an assumption that may not be justifiable. Due to this problem, it is not clear what is actually known about dynamic changes in intra-industry trade, based on the results of such studies. While high average income has consistently been strongly related to a high proportion of intra-industry trade, we do not know that as average income rises, intra-industry trade will necessarily increase. Therefore, time-series analysis would seem to be more useful if inference about the policy implications of growth of intra-industry trade is desired. The lack of empirical work in this area and the deficiencies of the existing studies make time series analysis an extremely promising area of research, as noted (but not pursued) by a number of authors. Therefore, this study attempts to fill some of this gap.

IV

Hypotheses on Intra-Industry Trade

The principal problem with the application of time-series analysis to intra-industry trade is that all the models of intra-industry trade are essentially static. A true solution to this problem must involve the derivation of a fully dynamic model of intra-industry trade. In the absence of such, the Helpman/Krugman and Bergstrand models, as well as the general formulations of the other empirical studies, provide some ground from which to discuss expected changes over time. The following five hypotheses will be tested using the methodology presented in the next chapter.

Hypothesis 1: *The share of intra-industry trade will increase as the difference in per capita incomes falls.*

This statement is based primarily on the familiar Linder (1961) hypothesis, which has figured prominently in the literature as the primary justification for the inclusion of income differences. The implication of the Linder hypothesis is that as nations' per capita incomes become more equal, demand structures are likely to become more similar. If it is further assumed that there is a preference for variety within product categories, as in the Helpman/Krugman models, intra-industry trade results.[1]

In the Bergstrand model, as preferences are not assumed to be homothetic, "wider per capita income differences can reduce the share of intra-industry trade here by widening taste differences, even after removing the effect of greater inequality in their capital-labour ratios".[2] Thus in this framework we should also observe more intra-industry trade when per capita incomes are about the same.

Hypothesis 2: *The share of intra-industry trade will rise as the difference in factor compositions falls.*

In the Helpman/Krugman model, which assumes that the production of differentiated goods is capital-intensive, it may easily be shown that a reallocation of factors from the (capital-rich) home country that changes relative endowments but not relative income will move some production of the differentiated good to the foreign country, and thus intra-industry trade will increase. This may also be shown in the Bergstrand model if the same assumption is made.

Additionally, increasing the dissimilarity in factor endowments must increase comparative cost advantages and thus increase non-overlapping trade. Ethier (1982) also suggests that intra-industry trade and factor mobility are complementary. That is, if factors of production move freely across borders, national capital/labor ratios may tend to be very similar in long-run equilibrium (depending, of course, on the extent of free trade and on the adjustment of wages and prices). Thus all remaining trade must be intra-industry in nature as cost differences disappear.

Hypothesis 3: *The share of bilateral intra-industry trade will increase as the average level of income increases.*

As the level of economic development increases and average incomes rise, consumers purchase more luxury goods. As assumed by Bergstrand, differentiated consumer goods are generally luxuries in consumption; thus as average income levels rise, relative consumption of X must rise. This increases the amount and proportion of X in the consumption bundle and thus the share of intra-industry trade will increase.

Hypothesis 4: *The share of bilateral intra-industry trade will increase as differences in the relative incomes of the trading partners falls.*

In the Helpman/Krugman model, the greatest volume of intra-industry trade arises when countries have identical incomes and identical factor endowments. When all goods are differentiated, relative country size (income) is the sole determinant of the volume of trade, implying that the more specialization there is in production, the more important the role of relative country size. The sense of this idea is that the volume of trade in differentiated goods is a function of the share of world income spent by each country. Since there is demand in each country for all varieties of each good, the maximum volume of trade in such goods occurs when the shares of each country in world spending are equal. Let the economic size of one country increase relatively, due to reallocation of capital and labor, which changes both capital/labor ratios and national income. The share of the rich nation in world spending increases, and there is increased intersectoral trade due to the difference in capital/labor endowments. For both these reasons, the share of intra-industry trade must decline.

Hypothesis 5: *The share of bilateral intra-industry trade will increase as the total size of the trading partners increases.*

As the total economic size of the 'world' increases, it is expected that it will be possible to trade more varieties of goods due to the increased opportunities for product differentiation and specialization.[3] This is due to the presumed increase in number and/or consumption of buyers in each country. If there are more (equally wealthy) consumers or if each consumer has more to spend and thus purchases more varieties, it will be profitable to produce a wider variety of goods. Under the assumed supply conditions, more firms will enter the market in each country. Therefore more varieties are produced and traded, increasing intra-industry trade (as long as there are some consumers of each type in each country).[4]

NOTES

[1] This can also arise from demand from variety in intermediate goods, as in Ethier (1982).

[2] Bergstrand (1990), p. 1221.

[3] Since Adam Smith, it has, of course, been well-known that specialization is limited by the size of the market. Marvel and Ray (1987) find support for this in an industry-specific framework, finding the share of intra-industry trade greatest in industries producing made-to-order intermediate goods with diverse customers.

[4] However, it is possible that there is a limit to this type of expansion of intra-industry trade, depending on the distribution of customers or the form of preference for variety. In each country is sufficiently large and the number of customers of each type is finite, with non-zero transportation costs, there may be some point at which the number of consumers in each economy is sufficiently large to support domestic industries producing every variety of good, and thus intra-industry trade may actually fall as total economic size increases.

V

Methodology and Data Sources

To test empirically the theoretical constructs of the previous section, it is necessary to first select an appropriate measure of intra-industry trade. The hypothesized independent variables and their expected signs are then discussed.

5.1 THE MEASUREMENT OF INTRA-INDUSTRY TRADE

This study is concerned with the bilateral share of intra-industry trade, which can be measured in different ways. Any reliable measure of the share of intra-industry trade must be trade-weighted; the principal debate is whether to adjust for overall trade imbalance. The motivation behind such adjustment is that the overall trade balance is influenced by macroeconomic variables that are likely to be somewhat irrelevant to intra-industry trade, such as interest rates, savings, investment, and government budget deficits. In the presence of a large trade imbalance, the share of intra-industry trade will tend to be understated to the extent that trade is also highly unbalanced for individual products.

Adjustments have been proposed by Grubel and Lloyd (1975) and Aquino (1979). The former simply adjusts the overall share by multiplying by a factor representing overall trade imbalance. The latter assumes that the imbalance in each category is proportionately related to the overall imbalance in manufactured goods,[1] and that the proportion is identical for each category. Both measures assume that all industries are affected identically by trade imbalance, a hypothesis that may not be justifiable. Either adjustment method is based on simplistic and arbitrary assumptions, and it has been argued that, all things considered, it is best to use unadjusted figures.[2] This study tests both measures, but unless Japan is included in the sample, there is little difference between the measures (see also Figures 6-9 in the following chapter). However, as discussed later, use of the adjusted measure may be preferable due to the effects of fluctuations of the value of the dollar on the trade balance and on dollar-denominated data.

As a measure of the share of intra-industry trade, following Balassa (1986), $SIIT_{jk}$ refers to the index of intra-industry trade between a pair of countries. This measure is adjusted for total trade imbalance as in Aquino (1979). An unadjusted measure simply removes the weighting factors from X^e and M^e. $SIIT_{jk}$ approaches 1 as intra-industry trade increases.

$$SIIT_{jk} = 1 - \{ \ \Sigma_i \ |X^e_{jki} - M^e_{jki}| \ / \ \Sigma_i \ (X^e_{jki} + M^e_{jki}) \} \qquad (5.1)$$

$$\text{where:} \quad X^e_{jki} = X_{jki} \{(X_{jk} + M_{jk})/2X_{jk}\}$$
$$M^e_{jki} = M_{jki} \{(X_{jk} + M_{jk})/2M_{jk}\}$$

5.2 SPECIFICATION OF THE MODEL

Due to deficiencies in early data, explained below, and the lack of capital stock data after 1987, the sample is restricted to 1965-1987. While it would be desirable to estimate equations separately for trade between the United States and each of the sample countries, the period is not sufficiently lengthy to allow reliable estimation. Preliminary estimation for each country showed high explanatory power, but individual parameters were generally not significant, the usual consequence of multicollinearity. With few observations and closely correlated independent variables, inference from the results of this procedure would be questionable at best. Thus the cross-sectional and time-series data is pooled to allow for sufficient length of sample.[3]

As the share of intra-industry trade (SIIT) ranges from 0 to 1, it is necessary to specify the model so that predicted values lie within this range. As no values are close to 0 or 1, a logit transformation is used.

$$\ln [SIIT_{it} / (1- SIIT_{it})] = \beta 'X_{it} + \varepsilon_{it} \quad\quad (5.2)$$
$$\varepsilon_{it} = \mu_i + \lambda_t + e_{it}$$

where i = country (i=1 to 4), t = time (t=1 to 23), and X is the matrix of explanatory variables, which consists of the absolute value of the difference in capital/labor ratios, the absolute value of the difference in per capita GDPs, average per capita GDP, the exchange rate, the difference in GDPs (discussed below), and a dummy variable for each country and each year.

As shown above, to allow for the differing fixed effects attributable to countries and years, the error term is expected to have three components, the country-varying element μ_i , the time-varying element λ_t , and e_{it} , which varies with both time and countries. e_{it} is assumed to be an independently and identically distributed random error with mean of zero and a constant variance, assumed to result from unsystematic errors, including measurement error. The appropriate estimation procedure for this type of model is to include dummy variables for countries and years, as specified above. The equation may then be estimated by ordinary least squares.[4]

Preliminary estimation, with the inclusion of dummy variables for countries and years, was tested for serial correlation, based on the appropriate Durbin-Watson (DW) statistic for pooled time-series/cross-sectional data sets.[5] As this statistic implicitly assumes constant error variance across groups, the sample was first checked for heteroskedasticity across countries. The appropriate likelihood test could not reject the hypothesis of homoskedasticity in either the four or five country sample.[6] Regardless of the set of countries selected, no evidence of first-order autocorrelation could be found.

Annual data on trade flows was collected from the United Nations Commodity Trade Statistics from 1965 to 1987. A major portion of the work involved in this study was the refinement of this data set. While this series began in 1951, prior to 1962 data was collected by 3-digit Standard International Trade Classification (SITC) code only. Collection under SITC Revision 2 began in 1962, but the figures for 1962-1964 are extremely low relative to following years, although the overall volume of trade did not change dramatically over the period. Due to this problem and other discrepancies suggestive of collection error, these years were omitted from the sample period. Although this data is publicly available, the United Nations collection and publication methods required extensive study and manipulation of the published data to obtain the appropriate figures for all relevant SITC codes.

As most intra-industry trade occurs in manufactured products, 4 digit subgroups of SITC 5-8 are used for trade flows to or from the U.S. and the five countries. Excluding agricultural goods has the additional advantage of virtually removing overlapping trade in homogeneous goods based on high transportation costs or different growing seasons. While many authors have selected only certain industries from SITC 5-8, there are two reasons to use all categories.

Firstly, shares of intra-industry trade are fairly invariant to choice of industries. Calculation of intra-industry trade with different choices of industries showed significant differences in levels only when a large number of industries was excluded.

Secondly, while there may be reasons for selecting or omitting certain industries based on raw materials requirements or manufacturing processes, any selection of this type is difficult to justify at the level of aggregation of this data and would tend to bias shares upward.

Additionally, this data is collected exclusively in dollar terms, and this presents a statistical problem. If the dollar value of imports exceeds the dollar value of exports both before and after exchange rate changes (as is the case in the majority of categories in this sample), and the dollar appreciates, then, ceteris paribus, the share of intra-industry trade will increase, even if there is no real difference in the quantity of units traded. Depending on the reasons for the exchange rate change, in a world of perfect adjustment, real trade volumes would change as well, and prices in one or both countries would be expected to be different. However, in a world that is characterized by somewhat sticky world prices and persistent deviations from purchasing power parity (as is well-documented in the related literature), it is not possible to assume that all such adjustments will take place or that adjustment will necessarily be complete. Thus rather than simply measuring a statistical artifact, this effect may also show some of the persistent effects of incomplete price adjustment.

Therefore, the exchange rate is included in all regressions in this study to control for the above problem as well as other related factors. The exchange rate is explicitly included in Bergstrand's theoretical model.[7] However, it is not possible to determine its expected sign, as there are two effects.

For example, consider the following simple equation for intra-industry trade in one industry:

$$IIT= 1 - [|X-M| / (X+M)] \tag{5.3}$$

The term in brackets is the share of non-intra-industry trade. An appreciation of the dollar should cause exports from the U.S. to its partner to decrease (as U.S. goods become more expensive overseas). Thus X unambiguously falls if denominated in dollars (and foreign demand is not perfectly inelastic). However, the quantity of U.S. imports should increase as their price in dollars has now fallen, *ceteris paribus*. The effect on M, the dollar value of imports, thus depends on the U.S. price elasticity of demand for imports. If the demand for imports is inelastic, the share of intra-industry trade must rise as the dollar appreciates.

Estimates of elasticities of import demand available do not yield a conclusion on this problem. Existing studies have produced wide array of estimates from inelastic to highly elastic. These elasticities are usually estimated for all imports, not for those from a specific partner as would be most useful here, and are sensitive to choice of goods. See Stern et al (1976) for a comprehensive survey; more recent studies do not seem to have reached any greater consensus as to the magnitude of these elasticities.

GDP, population, price indices, and exchange rates are found in International Financial Statistics, employment data in Quarterly Labor Statistics, and net capital flows and stocks in Flows and Stocks of Fixed Capital. For Japan, only gross capital stock data is available; to avoid distortion due to the size of the Japanese figure, a rate of depreciation equal to the average rate of depreciation in other countries is assumed.

As in Balassa and Bauwens (1987), the relative difference in economic sizes is measured by:

$$SIZEDIF = 1 + [w \ln w + (1-w) \ln (1-w)]/\ln 2 \tag{5.4}$$

where w = CONS /(CONS + CONS),

and CONS is real domestic consumption. This measure ranges from 0 to 1 and is a convex function of w. Conventional use of the absolute value of the difference tends to be greatly influenced by the size of the variables in each country. This is not as large a problem for such variables as capital/labor ratios and per capita GDPs, which tend to be of approximately the same magnitude. However for variables such as GDP, the size of the United States tends to bias the measure upward. The absolute value of the difference is also highly correlated with other income-related variables. The Balassa/Bauwens proxy shows a lower level of correlation and captures more of the characteristic desired, that is, the share of world income spent by consumers in one country, relative to the other.[8]

Bergstrand and others have also proposed a relationship between intra-industry trade and average GDP (as proxy for average size of markets) and between intra-industry trade and average capital-labor ratios (showing increased capital intensity, which should expand production of differentiated goods). These were omitted here as both variables were almost perfectly correlated with other independent variables and created serious estimation problems. The reasons for including average GDP are nearly identical to the rationale for average per capita GDP, and thus it does not appear necessary to include both.

Variable definitions are listed in Table 5. Descriptive statistics for the full sample and for each sample country paired with the United States are presented in Tables 6-11; these statistics will be discussed further in the following chapter.

Regression results for the full sample are summarized in Table 12. The model was also estimated for two different samples. The first excluded Japan, as Japan has notable structural differences from the other sample countries with regard to both intra-industry trade and to overall trade balance, and thus it is desirable to examine the robustness of parameter estimates between the two samples. The second estimation included only the European countries. These alternative results are presented in Tables 13 and 14 respectively.

For each set of countries, the estimated coefficients for some variables were not statistically significant. These equations were then re-estimated with these variables excluded; the results are presented in the last two columns in each related table.

TABLE 5: Variable definitions	
All variables are in logs.	
Name	Definition
LDIF	absolute value of the difference in capital/labor ratios in industry (Labor measured as hours worked per year)
KYPDIF	absolute value of the difference in per capita GDPs
AVYP	average per capita GDP
SIZED	absolute value of the difference in domestic consumption
TSIZE	total (bilateral) GDP
LRATE	exchange rate, dollars per unit of foreign currency

Table 6A: Descriptive Statistics for the Full Sample		
	MEAN	STD DEV
SIIT	0.358	0.123
YPDIF	0.125	0.198
KLDIF	0.511	0.255
AVYP	1.886	0.615
SIZED	0.472	0.209
TSIZE	8.934	1.656
RATE	1.827	1.972

Table 6B: Covariance Matrix for the Full Sample							
	SIIT	YPDIF	KLDIF	AVYP	SIZED	TSIZE	RATE
SIIT	0.015						
YPDIF	0.005	0.039					
KLDIF	-0.001	0.011	0.065				
AVYP	0.011	-0.063	0.067	0.379			
SIZED	0.017	0.031	-0.002	-0.053	0.017		
TSIZE	-0.146	-0.069	0.063	0.137	-0.227	2.744	
RATE	-0.187	-0.042	0.045	-0.068	-0.245	3.159	3.891

Table 6C: Correlation Matrix for the Full Sample							
	SIIT	YPDIF	KLDIF	AVYP	SIZED	TSIZE	RATE
SIIT	1.000						
YPDIF	0.197	1.000					
KLDIF	-0.002	0.228	1.000				
AVYP	0.148	-0.512	0.426	1.000			
SIZED	0.661	0.747	-0.055	-0.411	1.000		
TSIZE	-0.713	-0.209	0.149	0.134	-0.653	1.000	
RATE	-0.768	-0.107	0.089	0.056	-0.594	0.967	1.000

Table 7A: Descriptive Statistics for U.S./Canada		
	MEAN	STD DEV
SIIT	0.358	0.123
YPDIF	0.125	0.198
KLDIF	0.511	0.255
AVYP	1.886	0.615
SIZED	0.472	0.209
TSIZE	8.934	1.656
RATE	1.827	1.972

Table 7B: Covariance Matrix for U.S./Canada							
	SIIT	YPDIF	KLDIF	AVYP	SIZED	TSIZE	RATE
SIIT	0.008						
YPDIF	-0.001	0.001					
KLDIF	0.008	-0.001	0.025				
AVYP	0.036	-0.002	0.068	0.307			
SIZED	-0.002	0.001	-0.003	-0.008	0.001		
TSIZE	-0.012	-0.001	0.022	0.100	-0.002	0.033	
RATE	0.004	0.001	0.005	0.047	0.001	0.016	0.012

Table 7C: Correlation Matrix for U.S./Canada							
	SIIT	YPDIF	KLDIF	AVYP	SIZED	TSIZE	RATE
SIIT	1.000						
YPDIF	-0.606	1.000					
KLDIF	0.553	-0.835	1.000				
AVYP	0.702	-0.598	0.770	1.000			
SIZED	-0.606	0.950	-0.763	-0.528	1.000		
TSIZE	0.725	-0.556	0.755	0.989	-0.475	1.000	
RATE	0.371	0.030	0.300	0.775	0.103	0.786	1.000

Table 8A: Descriptive Statistics for U.S./France		
	MEAN	STD DEV
SIIT	0.342	0.066
YPDIF	0.030	0.023
KLDIF	0.464	0.275
AVYP	1.955	0.581
SIZED	0.406	0.059
TSIZE	8.483	0.201
RATE	1.688	0.217

Table 8B: Covariance Matrix for U.S./France							
	SIIT	YPDIF	KLDIF	AVYP	SIZED	TSIZE	RATE
SIIT	0.004						
YPDIF	-0.001	0.001					
KLDIF	0.009	-0.004	0.075				
AVYP	0.031	-0.009	0.122	0.337			
SIZED	-0.002	0.001	-0.008	-0.017	0.004		
TSIZE	0.010	-0.003	0.045	0.115	-0.005	0.040	
RATE	0.004	0.002	0.017	0.021	0.007	0.021	0.047

Table 8C: Correlation Matrix for U.S./France							
	SIIT	YPDIF	KLDIF	AVYP	SIZED	TSIZE	RATE
SIIT	1.000						
YPDIF	-0.583	1.000					
KLDIF	0.510	-0.651	1.000				
AVYP	0.813	-0.631	0.765	1.000			
SIZED	-0.485	0.951	-0.490	-0.481	1.000		
TSIZE	0.743	-0.614	0.817	0.985	-0.444	1.000	
RATE	0.312	0.322	0.283	0.457	0.508	0.475	1.000

Table 9A: Descriptive Statistics for U.S./Germany		
	MEAN	STD DEV
SIIT	0.314	0.035
YPDIF	0.026	0.029
KLDIF	0.524	0.261
AVYP	1.990	0.606
SIZED	0.335	0.075
TSIZE	8.227	0.176
RATE	1.010	0.272

Table 9B: Covariance Matrix for U.S./Germany							
	SIIT	YPDIF	KLDIF	AVYP	SIZED	TSIZE	RATE
SIIT	0.001						
YPDIF	0.001	0.001					
KLDIF	-0.003	-0.006	0.068				
AVYP	-0.005	-0.013	0.123	0.368			
SIZED	-0.001	0.002	-0.012	-0.024	0.006		
TSIZE	-0.002	-0.004	0.036	0.015	-0.006	0.031	
RATE	0.001	0.007	-0.053	-0.144	0.017	-0.039	0.074

Table 9C: Correlation Matrix for U.S./Germany							
	SIIT	YPDIF	KLDIF	AVYP	SIZED	TSIZE	RATE
SIIT	1.000						
YPDIF	0.021	1.000					
KLDIF	-0.324	-0.840	1.000				
AVYP	-0.231	-0.742	0.780	1.000			
SIZED	-0.066	0.899	-0.630	-0.524	1.000		
TSIZE	-0.298	-0.709	0.783	0.989	-0.466	1.000	
RATE	0.107	0.890	-0.747	-0.873	0.852	-0.826	1.000

Table 10A: Descriptive Statistics for U.S./United Kingdom		
	MEAN	STD DEV
SIIT	0.450	0.057
YPDIF	0.483	0.152
KLDIF	0.706	0.198
AVYP	1.556	0.596
SIZED	0.789	0.072
TSIZE	7.887	0.171
RATE	0.719	0.235

Table 10B: Covariance Matrix for U.S./United Kingdom							
	SIIT	YPDIF	KLDIF	AVYP	SIZED	TSIZE	RATE
SIIT	0.003						
YPDIF	-0.005	0.023					
KLDIF	0.003	-0.017	0.039				
AVYP	0.018	-0.088	0.076	0.356			
SIZED	-0.002	0.011	-0.007	-0.042	0.005		
TSIZE	0.005	-0.025	0.022	0.101	-0.011	0.029	
RATE	-0.008	0.034	-0.021	-0.125	0.016	-0.035	0.055

Table 10C: Correlation Matrix for U.S./United Kingdom							
	SIIT	YPDIF	KLDIF	AVYP	SIZED	TSIZE	RATE
SIIT	1.000						
YPDIF	-0.585	1.000					
KLDIF	0.219	-0.556	1.000				
AVYP	0.537	-0.976	0.640	1.000			
SIZED	-0.588	0.997	-0.517	-0.962	1.000		
TSIZE	0.523	-0.944	0.667	0.987	-0.926	1.000	
RATE	-0.563	0.959	-0.455	-0.895	0.971	-0.868	1.000

Table 11A: Descriptive Statistics for U.S./Japan		
	MEAN	STD DEV
SIIT	0.190	0.04
YPDIF	0.081	0.087
KLDIF	0.553	0.202
AVYP	1.880	0.662
SIZED	0.245	0.124
TSIZE	12.173	0.354
RATE	5.598	0.256

Table 11B: Covariance Matrix for U.S./Japan							
	SIIT	YPDIF	KLDIF	AVYP	SIZED	TSIZE	RATE
SIIT	0.001						
YPDIF	0.001	0.008					
KLDIF	0.001	-0.012	0.041				
AVYP	-0.009	-0.052	0.061	0.438			
SIZED	0.001	0.011	-0.016	-0.077	0.015		
TSIZE	-0.003	-0.03	0.039	0.229	-0.042	0.126	
RATE	0.004	0.018	-0.017	-0.158	0.029	-0.079	0.066

Table 11C: Correlation Matrix for U.S./Japan							
	SIIT	YPDIF	KLDIF	AVYP	SIZED	TSIZE	RATE
SIIT	1.000						
YPDIF	0.049	1.000					
KLDIF	0.078	-0.699	1.000				
AVYP	-0.373	-0.896	0.458	1.000			
SIZED	0.125	0.985	-0.620	-0.929	1.000		
TSIZE	-0.269	-0.943	0.540	0.977	-0.945	1.000	
RATE	0.404	0.811	-0.319	-0.930	0.893	-0.874	1.000

Table 12: Regressions 1 - 4 (Full Sample)				
	1	**2** (adjusted)	**3**	**4** (adjusted)
Constant	**2.660** (0.657)	**-1.757** (0.511)	**4.130** (1.073)	**-1.341** (0.414)
YPDIF	**-1.204** (2.860)**	**-0.611** (1.710)**	**-1.278** (3.065)**	**-0.632** (1.800)**
KLDIF	**-0.445** (1.317)*	**-0.436** (1.520)*	**-0.467** (1.377)*	**-0.443** (1.551)*
AVYP	**2.083** (2.899)**	**1.588** (2.606)**	**2.307** (3.335)**	**1.652** (2.833)**
SIZED	**-0.445** (1.142)	**-0.126** (0.381)	--	--
TSIZE	**-1.243** (3.142)**	**-0.554** (1.651)*	**-1.441** (4.039)**	**-0.610** (2.031)**
LRATE	**1.200** (6.185)**	**0.718** (4.363)**	**1.190** (6.129)**	**0.715** (4.373)**
n	115	115	115	115
DW	1.91	1.85	1.95	1.84
R²	.87	.86	.86	.85

Dependent variable: share of intra-industry trade, unadjusted or adjusted for trade imbalance. Sample is Canada, Japan, France, Germany, and Great Britain. * indicates significance at the 10% level. ** indicates significance at the 5% or 1% level. Country and time dummy variables are not shown.

Table 13:	Regressions 5 - 8 (without Japan)			
	5	**6** (adjusted)	**7**	**8** (adjusted)
Constant	**-8.714** (0.581)	**8.594** (0.657)	**-5.427** (3.128)**	**-3.351** (2.216)
YPDIF	**-0.637** (1.285)*	**-0.212** (0.493)	**-0.718** (1.553)*	--
KLDIF	**-1.020** (2.412)**	**-0.598** (1.623)*	**-1.005** (2.615)**	**-0.779** (2.387)**
AVYP	**2.167** (2.499)**	**1.783** (2.358)**	**2.458** (3.581)**	**1.556** (2.602)**
SIZED	**-0.317** (0.530)	**-0.188** (0.362)	--	--
TSIZE	**0.518** (0.265)	**1.531** (0.899)	--	--
LRATE	**0.967** (4.016)**	**0.687** (3.271)**	**1.003** (5.095)**	**0.529** (3.539)**
n	92	92	92	92
DW	2.08	2.06	1.96	1.97
R²	.75	.77	.76	.77

Dependent variable: share of intra-industry trade, unadjusted or adjusted for trade imbalance. Sample is Canada, France, Germany, and Great Britain. * indicates significance at the 10% level. ** indicates significance at the 5% or 1% level. Country and time dummy variables are not shown.

Table 14: Regressions 9 - 12 (European countries)				
	9	**10** **(adjusted)**	**11**	**12** **(adjusted)**
Constant	**-22.00** (1.483)*	**-2.176** (0.161)	**-8.322** (4.333)**	**-4.682** (2.723)**
YPDIF	**-0.710** (1.463)*	**-0.348** (0.785)	**-0.825** (1.805)**	--
KLDIF	**-0.953** (1.667)*	**-0.368** (0.706)	**-0.836** (1.534)*	**-0.668** (1.588)*
AVYP	**1.808** (2.272)**	**1.312** (1.809)*	**2.420** (3.871)**	**1.427** (2.552)**
SIZED	**-0.379** (0.656)	**-0.265** (0.501)	--	--
TSIZE	**1.807** (0.986)	**0.273** (0.163)	--	--
LRATE	**0.818** (3.752)**	**0.538** (2.704)**	**0.943** (5.373)**	**0.474** (3.129)**
n	69	69	69	69
DW	2.43	2.48	2.30	2.44
R^2	.77	.71	.74	.72
Dependent variable: share of intra-industry trade, unadjusted or adjusted for trade imbalance. Sample is France, Germany, and Great Britain. * indicates significance at the 10% level. ** indicates significance at the 5% or 1% level. Country and time dummy variables are not shown.				

NOTES

[1] Lincoln (1990) criticizes the use of manufactured goods alone in the adjustment factor as moving away from the original idea on which such adjustments are based and into microeconomic effects that are related to IIT and should thus be included.

[2] See Lincoln (1990), Appendix A, for further discussion.

[3] As in any time-series study, one concern is the stationarity of the dependent variable. While there is no a priori reason to expect that the share of intra-industry trade be nonstationary, a test for unit roots was performed for each country individually. It was possible to reject the null hypothesis of a unit root at the .01 significance level for all countries except France, and at the .05 level for France.

[4] See Judge et al (1985), Chapter 13, for discussion of the fixed-effect model procedures.

[5] The statistic is:

$$[\Sigma_i \Sigma_t (e_t - e_{t-1})^2] / [\Sigma_i \Sigma_t e_t^2]$$

See Bhargava et al (1982) for further details.

[6] See Maddala (1988), p. 163, or Feldstein (1967), for specification of this test.

[7] It was not, however, included when the model was estimated in Bergstrand (1990), and no reason is given for its omission.

[8] For the same reason, SIZEDIF was measured as difference in domestic consumption (CONS) rather than difference in GDPs.

VI

Empirical Evidence

6.1 THE DESCRIPTIVE STATISTICS

Examination of the descriptive statistics for the full sample and for individual countries (Tables 6-12) shows that while the mean share of intra-industry trade is 36%, individual countries vary from a low of 19% (Japan) to a high of 49% (Canada), and all variances are small. The lack of variability in the individual country data and small sample sizes with closely related variables yield correlations between the independent variables that are extremely high. Pooling the data largely removes this problem.

Plotting the movements in the share of intra-industry trade over time (Figures 6 and 7) shows that for all countries, the share of intra-industry trade has increased over this sample period if the trade balance adjustment is made. There is little difference in the trade-weighted versus unweighted shares with the exceptions of Germany and Japan, which are plotted separately in Figures 8 and 9 respectively. Only for Germany does the share of intra-industry trade decline in the unweighted measure.

Canada had a 25% share of intra-industry trade with the United States in 1965. By 1986, this had risen dramatically to 65%, the highest share in this sample group. This should not, of course, be surprising, as the U.S. and Canada are each other's largest trading partners and have cultures that are extremely similar. Additionally, some U.S. manufacturers have located plants in Canada, and vice-

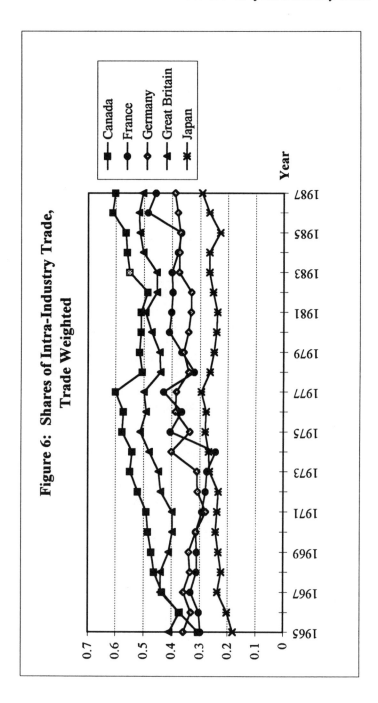

Figure 6: Shares of Intra-Industry Trade, Trade Weighted

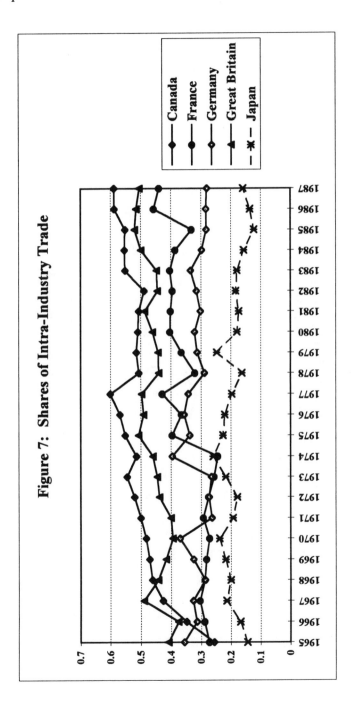

Figure 7: Shares of Intra-Industry Trade

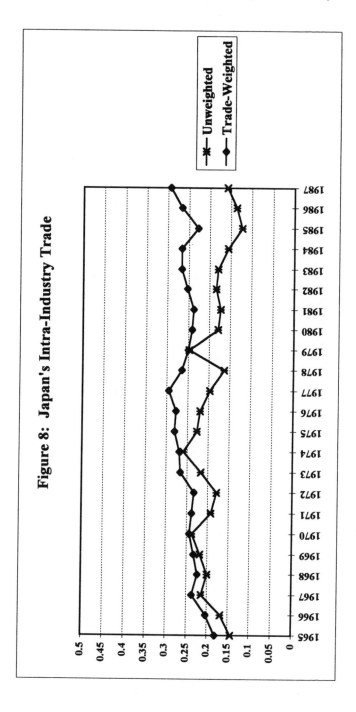

Figure 8: Japan's Intra-Industry Trade

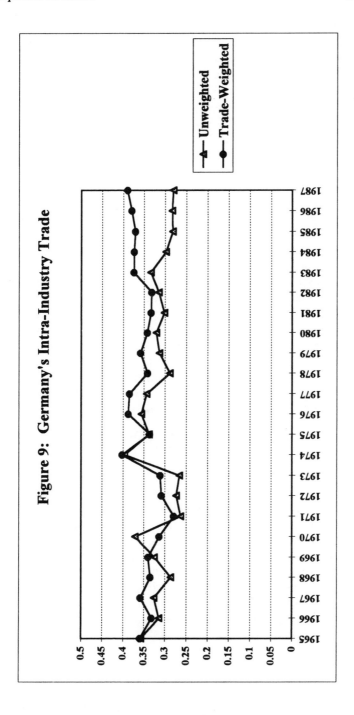

Figure 9: Germany's Intra-Industry Trade

versa; the recent North Atlantic Free Trade Agreement (NAFTA) is only likely to intensify this trend.

France and the United Kingdom show similar trends. France begins at 27% and rises to 38% by the end of the period. The United Kingdom begins at 41% and rises to 50%. Figures show a similar increase if the trade-weighting factor is used.

However, for Japan and Germany, results are somewhat different. For both countries, the United States trade deficits increased far more over the period, and thus there is a substantive difference between the adjusted and unadjusted figures.

Japan, which has an abnormally small share of intra-industry trade, begins at 14%, rising to 16%, based on unadjusted figures. With the trade balance correction, the share begins at 18% and rises to 29%. Reasons for this very low share of intra-industry trade will be discussed in the next section.

Only for Germany does the unadjusted share decline. In the 1965, the share was 35%, falling to 28% by the end of the period. Using the adjusted figures, the initial 35% rises to 38%, an insignificant difference. A number of factors could explain the absence of change and would require further investigation, but one explanation could be the relatively high wages in Germany, which have steadily driven up the cost of German product in the United States (and lowered the relative cost of competing U.S. good in Germany), which have made substitute goods less attractive to U.S. buyers.

6.2 THE REGRESSION RESULTS

In the five-country regressions (Table 13), results generally support the stated hypotheses. When the dependent variable is unadjusted for trade balance effects (Regressions 1 and 3), the coefficients of the explanatory variables have the expected signs and are significant, with two exceptions. The difference in economic sizes (SIZED) is not significant, and total economic size (TSIZE) is significant but has a negative sign. When the dependent variable is adjusted for trade imbalance, the results are, in general, statistically the same, although coefficients are slightly smaller in magnitude (Regressions 2 and 4). Estimation with the exclusion of insignificant variables yielded nearly identical results.

These results support the hypotheses that from 1965 to 1987, intra-industry trade has been influenced by both supply-side (KLDIF) and demand-side (YPDIF, AVYP) country characteristics in the predicted manner. Thus, supporting Bergstrand (1990), and unlike most of the previous country studies, this research shows the separate influence of capital and labor endowments on intra-industry trade. This lends empirical support to both the Bergstrand and Helpman/Krugman models. As KLDIF and YPDIF are positively correlated for the full sample, studies that have used per capita GNP differences as a proxy for capital/labor ratios have to some extent misinterpreted the separate effects of factor endowments and income differences on intra-industry trade.

At the same time, the influences of relative incomes and average development levels over time have been confirmed. This leads to the expectation that intra-industry trade will continue to increase as world economic integration becomes more complete. The falling difference in per capita GDP has increased intra-industry trade; the usual implication is that tastes are more similar where per capita incomes are similar, or that tastes are identical everywhere, but consumers with similar incomes will be able to purchase similar consumption bundles.

While the significance of the exchange rate may be a statistical artifact due to the methods of data collection, clearly its effect on this data cannot be ignored. It is not at all certain, based on these results, whether the significance of this variable is due to the nature of the data collection methods and thus is lacking in interesting economic implications, or whether it controls for the host of macroeconomic variables that influence relative prices, the trade balance, and therefore all types of trade. The t-statistic for the estimated coefficient for the exchange rate invariably falls when intra-industry trade is measured with adjustment for trade imbalance, although it is significant for all choices of countries.

To examine further the effects of the exchange rate, the equation was re-estimated excluding the late 70s and early 80s, years in which the dollar was appreciating against most currencies (choice of years depended on country). If the share of intra-industry trade was not adjusted for trade imbalance, the exchange rate was still marginally significant, but when the adjusted measure was used, no significant influence of the exchange rate could be found.

A test of parameter restrictions showed both the country and year dummy variables to be jointly significant. The year dummies are generally not significantly different from each other. The country dummies are generally not significant for the full sample. As these fixed-effect dummies have no interesting interpretation, they are omitted here.

It was hypothesized that total economic size would have a positive sign; the negative and significant results imply that, for the full sample, as total market sizes increased, intra-industry trade fell. This unexpected result may be due to the large size of markets involved and suggests that there is a limit to the expansion of intra-industry trade based on the distribution of customers or the form of preference for variety, or that the gains from specialization are small relative to natural and regulatory barriers to trade. If each country is sufficiently large and the number of customers of each type is finite, with non-zero transportation costs there is likely to be some point at which the number of consumers in each economy is sufficiently large to support domestic industries producing every variety of good, and thus the share of intra-industry trade may eventually begin to fall as total economic size increases and scale economies are exhausted.

However, examination of the data shows that only for Japan does the share of intra-industry trade appear to fall as total income increases, and only for Japan and Germany is the correlation between SIIT and TSIZE negative. As discussed below, this variable is only significant when Japan is included; in all other specifications, estimated coefficients are positive but never significant.

There has been much speculation as to the 'abnormally' low level of intra-industry trade between Japan and its major trading partners. In the past decade, the largest United States bilateral trade imbalance has been with Japan, and it is only with the Japanese shares that the trade balance adjustment appears to have much nominal effect on the intra-industry trade share. This effect becomes pronounced in the 1980s as the trade deficit increased (Figure 8). Also, two well-known 'stylized facts' are that Japan imports raw materials and exports capital or technology-intensive finished products and that Japan has often restricted imports that compete with domestic industries. This seems to have created persistent differences in Japan's share of intra-industry trade, although there appears to be an upward trend in the data for the last few sample years.

The model was estimated with the exclusion of Japan (Table 12); results were similar except that total size is now positive and not significant. The difference in per capita incomes was significant only for the unadjusted measure. Estimation with only the European countries (Table 13) showed only the exchange rate, capital/labor ratio difference, and average per capita income to be significant. As the sample countries have very similar but rising per capita incomes, this suggests that increased economic development will continue to increase intra-industry trade, but that taste differences may be playing less of a role. Differences in relative capital/labor endowments are also important. However, these differences are decreasing among developed countries, a trend that is likely to continue with the increased economic integration of the European Union.

The difference in country sizes (SIZED) is not significant in any sample, although the descriptive statistics for each country shows a high and negative correlation. This may be due to a continuing multicollinearity problem, as this variable is highly correlated with both per capita income differences and total size. While descriptive statistics show very high correlations for many of the independent variables for each country, these correlations drop dramatically for the entire sample with this exception.

When all results are considered, four overall observations may be made. Firstly, most of the expected relationships do exist. In particular, endowment differences and high average level of per capita income invariably are significant in explaining the share of intra-industry trade.

Secondly, these estimates are reasonably robust across choice of sample. Although estimated parameters do vary somewhat in magnitude across equations, the differences are not statistically significant in most cases.

Thirdly, use of the unadjusted measure of intra-industry trade tends to produce better results in the sense that more of the expected relationships can be found and significance levels are higher. As previously discussed, the rationale for making this adjustment at all is questionable, and its effects are uncertain. This suggests that the unadjusted measure may be preferable, especially if the exchange rate is included. However, for this group of countries there is little difference in unadjusted and adjusted measures. In Chapter VII, it will be shown that for a broader country group, there are far more substantive differences, and thus adjustment measures must still be considered.

Finally, perhaps the most striking observation that can be made from the results of this study is that while most of the expected relationships were found, these results are not particularly strong in the sense that only the exchange rate consistently shows a high t-statistic. This might be due to a lack of variability in the data in this set of rather homogenous countries. Nonetheless, it is surprising as it is intra-industry trade among countries with similar and high levels of development that this theory is engineered to explain. However, it also leads to the conclusion that intra-industry trade is driven by a complex set of interactions and conditions between countries. Unlike trade based on comparative advantage, there is no one simple factor that alone explains high intra-industry trade shares.

VII

Intra-Industry Trade and Economic Growth

While intra-industry trade is a well-documented phenomenon in cross-sectional studies of developed countries, little study has been made of newly-industrializing countries or of a broader range of sample countries. The objectives of this chapter are to examine the pattern of the share of intra-industry trade between the United States and nations at varying levels of development, using a larger number of countries than in the previous chapters; and to attempt to establish a relationship between intra-industry trade patterns and economic growth.

This work again follows the theoretical models of Helpman and Krugman (1985) and Bergstrand (1990), as presented in Chapter II. Thus the same hypothesized relationships as stated in Chapter IV should still exist. The estimation methodology is identical to that presented in Chapter V. The data employed is again bilateral trade by 4-digit SITC code between the United States and an expanded sample of 22 countries, consisting of both developing and developed nations. The 22 countries are Australia, Belgium, Brazil, Canada, Finland, France, Germany, Greece, Ireland, Israel, Italy, Japan, Korea, Mexico, the Netherlands, New Zealand, Norway, Portugal, Spain, Sweden, the United Kingdom, and Venezuela.

Data availability for the independent variables has restricted the choice of sample countries somewhat. While it would be desirable to include representatives of the very poor countries, adequate data does not exist for such variables as capital stocks.

Table 15: Intra-Industry Trade Shares, 22 country sample, unweighted		
	Mean	Standard Deviation
Australia	0.129	0.025
Belgium	0.173	0.121
Brazil	0.184	0.057
Canada	0.599	0.009
Finland	0.130	0.052
France	0.458	0.016
Germany	0.350	0.060
Greece	0.037	0.022
Ireland	0.309	0.164
Israel	0.251	0.161
Italy	0.256	0.078
Japan	0.210	0.045
Korea	0.158	0.047
Mexico	0.380	0.184
Netherlands	0.336	0.093
New Zealand	0.099	0.037
Norway	0.137	0.071
Portugal	0.091	0.057
Spain	0.188	0.035
Sweden	0.245	0.070
Switzerland	0.392	0.085
United Kingdom	0.508	0.003
Venezuela	0.134	0.047

Table 16: Intra-Industry Trade Shares, 22 country sample, trade weighted		
	Mean	Standard Deviation
Australia	0.221	0.123
Belgium	0.176	0.114
Brazil	0.215	0.078
Canada	0.543	0.050
Finland	0.141	0.046
France	0.458	0.000
Germany	0.443	0.047
Greece	0.054	0.014
Ireland	0.340	0.181
Israel	0.304	0.104
Italy	0.303	0.104
Japan	0.363	0.060
Korea	0.185	0.067
Mexico	0.382	0.170
Netherlands	0.373	0.100
New Zealand	0.105	0.036
Norway	0.148	0.054
Portugal	0.132	0.041
Spain	0.193	0.029
Sweden	0.303	0.105
Switzerland	0.413	0.106
United Kingdom	0.516	0.011
Venezuela	0.128	0.031

Table 17 : Average Annual Growth Rate of Intra-Industry Trade Share(%)		
	Unweighted	Trade-Weighted
Australia	4.28	62.58
Belgium	44.42	37.97
Brazil	47.97	66.26
Canada	1.14	-6.89
Finland	43.12	29.60
France	2.81	0.02
Germany	14.50	8.53
Greece	248.72	-11.05
Ireland	177.69	174.96
Israel	153.48	39.08
Italy	46.35	59.08
Japan	18.30	13.87
Korea	41.00	56.67
Mexico	118.50	104.58
Netherlands	41.96	41.31
New Zealand	38.32	21.48
Norway	58.91	50.51
Portugal	204.37	36.06
Spain	23.82	18.77
Sweden	40.54	53.86
Switzerland	28.65	27.79
United Kingdom	0.45	1.73
Venezuela	-18.07	4.68
Correlation with Average Income Growth: **Entire Sample = 15.6%** **Lower Income Countries = 25.4%**		

Once again, the share of intra-industry trade is measured both with and without trade weighting. While there is little difference in the measures for the highest income countries, there is a substantial difference for lower income nations.

Tables 15 and 16 show average share and standard deviation of intra-industry trade for each country, with and without adjustment for trade imbalance respectively. Highest shares are found for countries most similar (to the U.S.) in level of development (Canada, Japan, the majority of the European countries) and for those in close proximity to the United States (Canada, Mexico). Shares are far lower for most newly industrializing countries (South Korea, Brazil, Venezuela) and where distance and transportation may be an issue and/or there are relatively small manufacturing sectors (Australia, New Zealand).

Over time, intra-industry trade has increased for most of the sample countries (Table 17), although the growth rates vary widely.[1] It should be noted once again that while the magnitude of some of the change in intra-industry trade shares may appear small, to generate a change of even 1% requires a shift of millions of dollars worth of trade from inter- to intra-industry categories. Growth rates of share of intra-industry trade are generally higher for smaller, lower income countries. In the largest counties, most growth of this type of trade probably took place in the late 1970s and early 1980s (as shown in the previous data set); while the share is still increasing in these countries, further change is necessarily slow.

While, at this point, no suggestion is made as to the direction of causality, there is an approximately 15% correlation between income growth and increase in the share of intra-industry trade for the entire sample (regardless of which measure of intra-industry trade is used). This figure is slightly for the lower income countries, at approximately 25%. Some hypotheses about this relationship are presented at the end of this chapter.

As in the previous chapter, relationships were estimated using a fixed-effects model.

$$\ln [SIIT_{it} / (1 - SIIT_{it})] = \beta' X_{it} + \varepsilon_{it} \qquad (7.1)$$
$$\varepsilon_{it} = \mu_i + \lambda_t + e_{it}$$

where i=country (i=1 to 4), t=time (t=1 to 23), and X_{it} is the matrix of explanatory variables, which consists of the absolute value of the difference in capital/labor ratios, the absolute value of the difference in per capita

GDPs, average per capita GDP, the exchange rate, the difference in GDPs (discussed below), and a dummy variable for each country and each year. As shown above, to allow for the differing fixed effects attributable to countries and years, the error term is expected to have three components, the country-varying element μ_i, the time-varying element λ_t, and e_{it}, which varies with both time and countries. e_{it} is assumed to be an independently and identically distributed random error with mean of zero and a constant variance, assumed to result from unsystematic errors, including measurement error, and is uncorrelated both across countries and over time. The estimation procedure for this type of model is to include dummy variables for countries and years, as specified above. The equation may then be estimated by generalized least squares.[2] Preliminary estimation showed no evidence of serial correlation or heteroskedasticity.

Annual data on trade flows is collected from the United Nations Commodity Trade Statistics from 1987 to 1990. 1987 was the first year in which the United Nations collected data by SITC Version 3, a substantially more disaggregated form than previous versions. Thus these figures are in a sense not directly comparable with those in the previous chapter; with more disaggregated data, intra-industry trade shares should be lower to the extent that the more aggregated codes may have allowed for some miscategorization of similar products. However, the shares are, if anything, higher on average than the 1986 observations from the previous sample.

While it would be desirable to estimate equations separately for trade between the United States and each of the sample countries, the period is not sufficiently lengthy to allow reliable estimation. Therefore the cross-sectional and time-series data is again pooled to allow for an adequately large sample size.[3] All methodology is identical to that used in the previous estimations; thus further repetition of the details is omitted here.

Regression results are reported in Table 18. The model was estimated for the full panel (Regression 13); results reported have the trade-weighted share of intra-industry trade as the dependent variable. Estimation with unweighted shares gave virtually identical results, and they are thus omitted here. In the 22-country sample, the high correlation between average per capita income and total economic size caused multicollinearity problems; as total size was never significant, it was removed.

While this sample contains no countries of truly low income nations, Brazil, Mexico, Venezuela, Greece, Spain, Finland, and Portugal have significantly lower per capita GDPs than the rest of the sample.

Table 18: Regressions 13-15, Large Sample			
	13	**14** **(low income)**	**15** **(comparison)**
Constant	**33.717** (4.773)**	**-1.757** (0.511)	**2.660** (0.657)
KLDIF	**-0.032** (-3.074)**	**-0.436** (1.520)*	**-1.204** (2.860)**
YPDIF	**-0.003** (-3.281)**	**-0.611** (1.710)*	**-0.445** (1.317)*
AVYP	**5.716** (5.002)**	**1.588** (2.606)**	**2.083** (2.899)**
SIZED	**-24.507** (-4.573)**	**-0.216** (3.609)**	**-0.445** (1.142)
TSIZE	--	**0.554** (3.045)**	**-1.243** (3.142)**
n	92	28	115
DW	2.30	1.85	1.91
R²	0.81	0.71	0.87
Dependent variable: share of intra-industry trade adjusted for trade imbalance. * indicates significance at the 10% level. ** indicates significance at the 5% or 1% level. Country and time dummy variables are not shown.			

A separate equation was estimated for this lower-income subgroup (Regression 14). The greater variability in the small sample allowed the inclusion of total size which is far less closely correlated with average per capita income for this group.

In the third column is reported analogous results of from the previous sample, for comparison purposes. Regression 15 corresponds with Regression 1 in Chapter V.

In the full-sample regression (13), results support the stated hypotheses. The coefficients of the explanatory variables have the expected signs and are highly significant. In fact, this equation is an 'improvement' on the previous results in the sense that the t-statistics are all greater in magnitude. In the low-income sample, all variables are significant and have the expected signs; however, the small sample size makes the reliability of this estimation somewhat lower.

The parameter estimates are also considerably different in magnitude from those reported for the five-country sample. There are a variety of possible reasons for this, but likely culprits are the SITC revisions or perhaps structural changes over time.[4]

These results again support the hypotheses that from 1987 to 1990, intra-industry trade has been influenced by both supply-side (KLDIF) and demand-side (AVYP, TSIZE) country characteristics. Thus this sample again confirms the separate influence of capital and labor endowments on intra-industry trade, lending further empirical support to both the Bergstrand and Helpman/Krugman models.

The influences of relative incomes and average development levels are again substantial. The addition of some newly industrializing countries tends to support the previous expectation that intra-industry trade would continue to increase as world economic integration becomes more complete. In particular, the highly significant influence of average per capita incomes in both the full-sample and low-income regressions combined with the correlation between income growth and intra-industry trade shares suggests a continuing relationship between this type of trade and economic growth and development.

Clearly, the expectation is that as income increases, intra-industry trade shares should increase due to the more-than-proportional expected growth in demand for differentiated (luxury) goods. However, there may also be a secondary feedback effect. Increased growth leads to increased domestic consumer demand, but in less-developed countries in which growth has been primarily in agricultural sectors, supply increases have tended to worsen terms of trade due to the inelastic demand for such products. The extreme case is immiserizing growth, in which the worsening of the terms of trade actually lowers domestic consumption possibilities. However, with manufacturing growth directed at export markets, this terms of trade effect is unlikely to occur. If anything, terms of trade may improve, leading to further consumption, further growth, and further increases in the share of intra-industry trade.

Additionally, as discussed further in the following chapter, intra-industry trade may carry with it fewer structural readjustment problems, and thus there is less of an incentive for protection. There is concurrently less need to devote domestic resources to smoothing structural readjustment problems, and therefore more productive investments can be made.

The significant effect of total market size in the lower-income regression might suggest that targeting development efforts toward export promotion may be more effective than import substitution policies. That is, absent a large home market, more domestic industries (and thus varieties of goods) may develop where there is a large trading partner to allow firms to achieve a sufficiently large size to exploit economics of scale.

These results should be considered preliminary. Ideally, at least ten more years should be added to the sample as well as a broader spectrum of countries. The sample is not sufficiently long to allow causality tests or any further examination of the hypotheses suggested above, and the nature of the SITC revisions makes simply extending the sample by using the pre-1987 data years problematic.

NOTES

[1] In fact, with the unadjusted measure, Germany's intra-industry trade share appears to have fallen in recent years.

[2] See Judge et al (1985), Chapter 13, for discussion of the fixed-effect model procedures. All equations were estimated using RATS.

[3] As in any time-series study, one concern is the stationarity of the dependent variable. However, there is no *a priori* reason to expect that there share of intra-industry trade would be nonstationary, and the length of the time-series is too short to allow a test for unit roots.

[4] Differences between the two data sets do not permit testing of the structural change hypothesis, at least through a standard Chow test.

VIII

Conclusions and Future Directions

This study has discussed and tested hypotheses on the share of intra-industry trade. The results support the Helpman/Krugman and Bergstrand models of trade in structurally competitive markets in the presence of economies of scale. Separate influences of relative incomes and factor endowments have been found, both over time and for a broad sample of countries, thus improving on the specification of empirical tests in the previous literature.

Additionally, the major influences found in earlier country studies, influence of per capita income differences and average per capita incomes, do hold both over time and for a wide range of countries. This connects the somewhat disjointed results from the variety of previous studies and yields an overall picture of what we know about the influences on intra-industry trade at this time, at least among developed economies.

Finally, a broader range of sample countries was included; the expected relationships hold again, even more strongly, when a wider range of countries is considered.

Based on this evidence, what can we conclude about the phenomenon of intra-industry trade, and why is it of major importance to understanding world trade? As the world economy becomes ever more integrated, and factors of production are more mobile worldwide, nations, particularly at high income levels, become increasingly alike in terms of factor endowments. Some 25% of world trade can now be counted as intra-industry in nature, and it is certain that this will only increase. At the same time, the 'rules' of the trade game are changing. While the General Agreement on Tariffs and Trade (GATT) has lowered average tariff rates worldwide, in many cases other forms of trade barriers and protection have taken their place. National governments are increasingly concerned with the creation of strategic trade policies to attempt to improve national competitiveness.

However, intra-industry trade may not cause the same types of national problems that have led to this rush toward protection and strategy. Unlike comparative advantage based trade, intra-industry trade can be welfare-enhancing for all national groups. For example, importing in general involves gain to domestic consumers (through lower prices) but losses to domestic producers (through lower prices and reduced sales). While the gains to the country as a whole are expected to exceed the loss to the producers, the concentration of the losses to the producers on a few firms and resulting structural readjustment costs lead to pressure for protection.

But intra-industry trade is likely to be a win-win situation. Domestic consumers still gain through lower prices (and greater variety of products) while domestic producers gain as well by exporting their varieties, increasing sales, and possibly achieving greater economies of scale. In this case, protection is clearly counterproductive, particularly if retaliation is probable.

In order to further understand such trade, it would be desirable to include bilateral trade flows between all sample countries rather than just with the United States. Bilateral intra-industry trade shares for the European countries are known to be much higher with each other than with the United States, for example. It is also probable that there is much more intra-industry trade between developing countries than between such nations and the developed world, since, as hypothesized earlier, relatively more intra-industry trade should take place among countries with similar levels of development. Results in Balassa (1986c) weakly support this idea. However, the abysmal state of data collection in many such countries has made this very difficult. In particular, capital stock data is unobtainable for many countries at this time. Also, the sheer volume of data required for a truly complete study is daunting at best.

Additionally, little work has been done on the impact of changing institutional structures, such as tariffs and foreign direct investment. Foreign direct investment (FDI) and any export activity could in theory be either substitutes or complements. That is, firms may directly invest rather than exporting, or conversely, the existence of foreign subsidiaries may increase exporting due either to supplying of parts to the subsidiary (which would not necessarily increase intra-industry trade) or because of facilitated access to markets in the foreign country. Caves (1981) thus argues that the greater the extent of FDI, the less intra-industry trade will be observed. Agmon (1979) suggests that intra-industry is the precursor of foreign direct investment. Investing in a foreign market is costly, and information about that market may not be readily available. Thus companies will export to gain information about markets; investment will take place when the marginal benefits of exporting have been exhausted. However, Lipsey and Kravis (1982) have found a complementary relationship.

Likewise, increased imports or concerns about future imports or trade deficits might induce increased protectionist measures to protect domestic markets, traditionally tariffs. However, it is possible that increased imports of intra-industry trade related goods could result in the opposite effect. Marvel and Ray (1987) argue that intra-industry trade has a negative effect on the level of protection, since industries are less likely to seek protection if they fear retaliation. Therefore, intra-industry trade may induce falling trade barriers. However, firms are more likely to enter industries in which trade barriers are lower (due to increased profit opportunities), and an increased number of product varieties will increase intra-industry trade. Thus falling trade barriers may induce intra-industry trade.

However, the lack of time-series data or suitable proxies for either of these variables has made this impossible at this time, although refinement in collection methods may improve this in the future.

Study of intra-industry trade patterns for the broad sample of countries have suggested that there reasons to believe that export-led development strategies, focusing on differentiated goods, may be more effective in spurring economic growth than import substitution policies. Intra-industry trade may also have some feedback effect on economic growth due to accelerating demand for luxury goods. These relationships must be further explored before any real conclusions can be drawn, but there are promising indications for continued study.

Bibliography

Abd-el-Rahman, K.S., "Hypotheses concernant le role des advantages specifiques des firmes dans l'explication des echanges croises des produits similaires," *Revue D'Economie Politique*, 97(2), 1987, 165-192.

_____, "Firms' competitive and national comparative advantages as joint determinants of trade composition," *Weltwirtschaftliches Archiv*, 1991, 127, 83-97.

Agmon, Tamir, "Direct Investment and Intra-Industry Trade: Substitutes or Complements?," in H. Giersch, (ed.), *On the Economics of Intra-Industry Trade*, Tübingen: J.C.B. Mohr, 1979, 49-62.

_____, and Hirsch, S., "Multinational corporations and the developing economies: potential gains in a world of imperfect markets and uncertainty," *Oxford Bulletin of Economics and Statistics*, 1979, 41, 333-44.

Anderson, James, "A Theoretical Foundation for the Gravity Equation," *American Economic Review*, 69(1), 1979, 106-116.

Aquino, Antonio, "Intra-Industry Trade and Inter-Industry Specialization as Concurrent Sources of International Trade in Manufactures," *Weltwirtschaftliches Archiv*, 1978, 114, 275-96.

Balassa, Bala, "The Determinants of Intra-Industry Specialization in United States Trade," *Oxford Economic Papers*, 1986a, 38, 220-233.

_____, "Intra-Industry Specialization: A Cross-Country Analysis," *European Economic Review*, 1986b, 30, 27-42.

_____, "Intra-industry trade among exporters of manufactured goods," in D. Greenaway and P.K.M. Tharakan, (eds.) *Imperfect Competition and International Trade: The Policy Aspects of Intra-Industry Trade*. Brighton: Wheatsheaf Press, 1986c.

_____, and Bauwens, Luc, "Comparative Advantage in Manufactured Goods in a Multi-country, Multi-industry and Multi-factor Model," in T. Peeters, P. Praet, and P. Reding, (eds.)

International Trade and Exchange Rates in the Late Eighties, Amsterdam, 1985, 31-52.

_____, "Intra-Industry Specialization in a Multi-Country and Multi-Industry Framework," *Economic Journal,* 97, 1987, 923-939.

_____, "Inter-Industry and Intra-Industry Specialization," *Weltwirtschaftliches Archiv,* 124(2), 1988, 1-13.

Baldwin, R.E., "Determinants of trade and foreign investment: further evidence" *Review of Economics and Statistics,* 1979, 71, 143-53.

Bergstrand, J.H., "Measurement and determinants of intra-industry international trade," in P.K.M. Tharakan, (ed.) Intra-industry Trade: Empirical and Methodological Aspects. Amsterdam: North-Holland 1983.

_____, "The Generalized Gravity Equation, Monopolistic Competition, and the Factor-Proportions Theory of International Trade," *Review of Economics and Statistics,* 1989, 71, 143-53.

_____, "The Heckscher-Ohlin-Samuelson Model, the Linder Hypothesis and the Determinants of Bilateral Intra-Industry Trade," *Economic Journal,* 1990, 100, 1216-1229.

Bhargava, A., L. Franzini, and W. Narendranathan, "Serial Correlation and the Fixed Effects Model," *Review of Economic Studies,* 1982, 44, 533-549.

Brander, James, "Intra-Industry Trade in Identical Commodities," *Journal of International Economics,* 1981, 11, 1-14.

_____, and Krugman, Paul "A reciprocal dumping model of international trade," *Journal of International Economics,* 1983, 13, 313-21.

Caves, R.E., "Intra-industry trade and market structure in the industrial countries" *Oxford Economic Papers,* 1981, 33, 203-23.

Dixit, A., and Norman, V., *The Theory of International Trade.* Cambridge: Cambridge University Press, 1980.

Ethier, Wilfred, "Internationally Decreasing Costs and World Trade," *Journal of International Economics,* 1979, 9, 1-24.

_____, "National and International Returns to Scale in the Modern Theory of International Trade," *American Economic Review,* 1982, 72, 389-405.

Falvey, Rodney E., "Commercial Policy and Intra-Industry Trade," *Journal of International Economics,* 1981, 11, 495-511.

Feldstein, M.S., *Economic Analysis for the Health Care Industry.* Amsterdam: North-Holland , 1967.

Flam, Harry, and Helpman, Elhanan, "Vertical Product Differentiation and North-South Trade," *American Economic Review*, 1987, 77, 810-22.

Giersch, H., (ed) *On the Economics of Intra-Industry Trade.* Tübingen: J.C.B. Mohr, 1979.

Graham, Edward, and Krugman, Paul, *Foreign Direct Investment in the United States.* Washington: Institute for International Economics, 1989.

Gray, H. Peter, "Intra-industry Trade: An 'Untidy' Phenomenon," *Weltwirtschaftliches Archiv*, 124 (2), 1988, 211-229.

Greenaway, D. and Tharakan, P.K.M., (eds.) *Imperfect Competition and International Trade: The Policy Aspects of Intra-Industry Trade.* Brighton: Wheatsheaf Press, 1986.

Greenaway, David, and Milner, Chris, *The Economics of Intra-Industry Trade.* Great Britain: Basil Blackwell Ltd., 1986.

Greenaway, D., Hine, R., and Milner C., "Vertical and Horizontal Intra-Industry Trade: A Cross Industry Analysis for the United Kingdom," *Economic Journal*, 1995, 105, 1505-1518.

_____, "Intra-Industry Trade: Current Perspectives and Unresolved Issues," *Weltwirtschaftliches Archiv*, 123(1), 1987, 39-57.

Grubel, Herbert G., and Lloyd, P.J., *Intra-Industry Trade: The Theory and Measurement of International Trade in Differentiated Products.* New York: Wiley and Sons, 1975.

Helpman, Elhanan, "International Trade in the Presence of Product Differentiation, Economies of Scale, and Monopolistic Competition," *Journal of International Economics*, 1981, 11, 305-340.

_____, "International Trade in Differentiated Middle Products," in K. Jugenfelt and D. Hague (eds.), *Structural Adjustment in Developed Open Economies.* London: Macmillan Press, 1985, 3-23.

_____, "Imperfect Competition and International Trade: Evidence from Fourteen Industrial Countries," *Journal of Japanese and International Economies*, 1987, 1, 62-81.

_____, and Krugman, Paul, *Market Structure and Foreign Trade.* Cambridge, Mass: M.I.T. Press, 1985.

Judge, George, Griffiths, W.E., Hill, R. Carter, Lutkepohl, Helmut, and Lee, Tsoung-Chao, *The Theory and Practice of Econometrics*. New York: Wiley and Sons, 1985.

Kravis, Irving, and Robert Lipsey, "The Location of Overseas Production and Production for Export by U.S. Multinational Firms," *Journal of International Economics*, 1982, 12, 201-223.

Krugman, Paul, "A Model of Innovation, Technology Transfer, and the World Distribution of Income," *Journal of Political Economy*, 1979a, 87, 253-266.

_____, "Increasing Returns, Monopolistic Competition, and International Trade," *Journal of International Economics*, 1979b, 9, 469-479.

_____, "Intraindustry Specialization and the Gains from Trade," *Journal of Political Economy*, 1981, 89, 959-973.

_____, "New Theories of Trade Among Industrial Countries," *American Economic Review*, 1983, 73, 343-347.

_____, "Scale Economies, Product Differentiation, and the Pattern of Trade," *American Economic Review*, 1980, 70, 950-959.

Lancaster, Kelvin, "Intra-Industry Trade Under Perfect Monopolistic Competition," *Journal of International Economics*, 1980, 10, 151-175.

Lincoln, Edward J., *Japan's Unequal Trade*. Washington: Brookings Institute, 1990.

Linder, S.B., *An Essay On Trade and Transformation*. New York: John Wiley, 1961.

Loertscher, Rudolf, and Wolter, Frank, "Determinants of Intra-Industry Trade: Among Countries and across Industries," *Weltwirtschaftliches Archiv*, 1980, 116, 280-293.

Maddala, G.S., *Introduction to Econometrics*. London: Macmillan Press, 1988.

Marvel, Howard P., and Ray, Edward John, "Intraindustry Trade: Sources and Effects on Protection," *Journal of Political Economy*, 1987, 95, 1278-1291.

Milner, Chris, "Weighting Considerations in the Measurement and Modeling of Intra-Industry Trade," *Applied Economics*, 1988, 20, 295-301.

Niroomand, Farhang, "Inter versus Intra-Industry Trade: A Note on U.S. Trends, 1963-1980," *Weltwirtschaftliches Archiv*, 1988, 124, 337-340.

Pagoulatos, E. and Sorensen, R. "Two-way international trade: an econometric analysis," *Weltwirtschaftliches Archiv*, 111, 1979, 454-65.

Peeters, T., Praet, P., and Reding, P., (eds.) *International Trade and Exchange Rates in the Late Eighties*. Amsterdam, 1985.

Ray, Edward John, "U.S. Protection and Intra-Industry Trade: The Message to Developing Countries," *Economic Development and Cultural Change*, 40, No.1, October 1991, 169-87.

Stern, Robert M., Francis, Jonathan, and Schumacher, Bruce, *Price Elasticities in International Trade*. London, Macmillan Press, 1976.

Tharakan, P.K.M., (ed.) *Intra-industry Trade: Empirical and Methodological Aspects*. Amsterdam: North-Holland, 1983.

Vona, Stefano, "On the Measurement of Intra-Industry Trade: Some Further Thoughts," *Weltwirtschaftliches Archiv*, 127 (4), 1991, 678-700.

Index